TRADING

This book includes:

Swing trading for beginners + Swing trading strategies that will guide you step by step towards financial freedom, through proven strategies

Mark Make

Table of Contents

SWING TRADING *FOR* BEGINNERS

SWING TRADING STRATEGIES

SWING TRADING
For
BEGINNERS

The guide on how to use proven strategies on options, forex, stocks with technical analysis, money management and market psychology. Achieve financial freedom.

Mark Make

INTRODUCTION

Most trading is boiled down to two types, wealth trading and trading for income. Swing traders are usually all about income trading. But for reference, we can look at wealth building style, or core trading, which is over weeks, and more often months, for longer-term accounts that are not time sensitive.

It can be important though to look at wealth building style, for perspective on the long-term market. To trade the market successfully, remember you're competing against experienced traders, so build up your own experience slowly. If you treat trading as a journey, that is a better mindset than trying to make money fast.

Obviously, everyone wants to make money. However, risking just one percent of your capital per trade will help you build experience and learn without dissipating your capital. Realize that you may have more losses than winners. In swing trading, you have to be thinking 100 trades ahead, and how to capitalize over the average on those 100 trades. To meet your swing trading goals, you need a strategy and the discipline to follow it. To be consistent, you need to know when to adapt.

That might sound like a contradiction, but it's not. Adapting doesn't mean you must change your trading plan. Adapting means you need to understand when to step on the gas and when to slow down. It means learning when to be in cash and when to add aggressively to winning positions. Inexperienced swing traders often believe that following a strategy is a black and white process. When I say adapt, I don't mean change your strategy. It is implying that you should adjust how you apply it.

One giant psychological hurdle to overcome is believing every trade is the same. It's simply not true. Some trades have a higher probability and should be managed differently. To succeed, you need to know what these scenarios look like, so you are ready to make quality decisions. You need to prepare yourself with a decision-making process before it happens. It's also important not to get caught up in comparing yourself to experienced/professional traders on Wall Street who claim to be making extraordinary profits on a consistent basis. When you're just starting out, the entire process should really be more of a competition with yourself – a focus on steady personal growth.

CHAPTER 1:
WHAT IS SWING TRADING.

What is Swing Trading?

It is a style of trading that attempts to catch benefits a securities trading inside one to four days of the period. It is likewise named as a momentary pattern following trading s. Investopedia Explains Swing Trading: To spot circumstances in which a stock or item has super potential to make developments in a shorter period outline, the dealer or the financial specialist must act carefully and quickly. This is predominantly utilized by the home brokers and the informal investors. Huge foundations for the most part trading measure that are too huge to move all through products quickly. In addition, the merchant or the financial specialist is fit for workaholic behavior the momentary stock developments and that likewise with no challenge with the huge and effective speculators. Swing merchants generally utilize specialized examination to view the stocks and items which are accessible in momentary value motivation. Such brokers are not intrigued by the crucial estimations of the offers, rather, are keen on realizing the value patterns and different examples. For what reason is Swing Trading the Preferred Approach? Swing trading is the best proficient methodology towards profiting and money in the entire financial trading. Continuously see the cost from where the stock diagrams start and where it closes. This is the situation of the customary financial specialist and the merchant. Notwithstanding sitting tight for a really long time periods for any stock or product to move in the normal course, you ought to duplicate your advantages simultaneously and that likewise with both long and short trading s. About $10,000 or more can be earned on the off chance that you trading the all over swings in contrast with the purchasing and holding the stock. In addition, swing trading is superior to anything the day trading in light of the fact that it is compelling than the day trading style, and even the cost related the business set up is additionally low on the grounds that the commissions are not rendered day by day. The swing dealers likewise have the chance to share among the more critical pieces of the value developments.

Swing Trading May be Right for you if: If any of the accompanying explanations portray your trading yields, Swing trading may demonstrate to be directly for you: You are disappointed with the low back up qualities on the purchase and-hold ventures and imagine that there is another better way. Swing trading will be all the more stuffing for you on the off chance that you won't keep a track on the business sectors entire day. Here and there you may feel dull and depleted, however you should work in a similar issue. It is certainly for you on the off chance that you have had the option to realize that you can profit just when you will apply your trading s inverse bearings for all your initial trading s of the stocks and wares.

What Are Its Benefits

The way toward swing trading has turned into a viral stock trading procedure utilized by numerous brokers over the market. This style of trading has demonstrated to be exceptionally effective for some dedicated stocks and Forex merchants. Customarily swing trading has been characterized as a progressively theoretical system as the positions are typically purchased and held for the merchant's foreordained time period. These time allotments could go somewhere in the range of two days to a couple of months. The objective of the swing broker is to recognize the pattern either up or down and place their trading s the most favorable position. From that point, the dealer will ride the heading to what they decide as the depletion point and sell for a benefit. Regularly, swing brokers will use a wide range of specialized markers that will enable them to have a progressively worthwhile likelihood when making their trading s. Shorter-term brokers don't really will in general swing trading as they incline toward holding positions for the duration of the day and practicing them before the end of the market. Swing trading methodology uses time, and it is this time is the obstacle factor for a long-time broker. Regularly there is an excessive amount of hazard engaged with the end of the market and that a broker won't acknowledge this hazard.

The qualification of swing trading is a wide subject in that it has various impacts from a huge number of various trading procedures. These trading techniques are interesting and have their separate hazard profiles. Swing trading can be a fantastic route for a market member to improve their specialized examination abilities further while enabling them to give more consideration to the crucial side of trading. Numerous fruitful swing merchants have been known to utilize a Bollinger band procedure as a device to help them in entering and leaving positions. Obviously, for a swing broker to be fruitful at the arrangement, they should have a high fitness for deciding the present market pattern and setting their situations by that pattern. It makes a swing merchant note great to put a short post with the arrangement of holding for an all-inclusive period in a market that is drifting upwards. The general subject here is that the objective of the dealers ought to be to build their likelihood of progress while restricting or disposing of hazard. The swing dealer's most noticeably terrible foe is that of a sideways or in a functioning business sector. Sideways value activity will stop a swing broker cold in their tracks as there is no common pattern to key off of.

CHAPTER 2:
THE BASICS OF SWING TRADING.

Now, it is time to move on and get to some of the basics about doing an actual swing trade. We are going to take a look at some of the steps that you need to take in order to enter the market, the types of positions that you can choose to take, and even how to take each of the positions that you choose. This will help you to get set up when it is time to do that first trade with this kind of trading strategy!

Choosing to Buy Long or Sell Short

The price of a stock is going to do one of three things at a given time. It will either go down, go up, or it will move sideways. When you enter into the market as a swing trader, you are expecting that the stock is going to either go up or it will go down. If you think that the stock will see an increase in its price, then they will purchase the stock. This move is going to be considered "going long" or having a "long position" in that stock. For example, if you are long 100 shares of Facebook Inc., it means that you purchased 100 shares of this company and you are making the prediction that you will be able to sell them at a higher price later on and earn a nice profit.

That one is pretty easy to understand, but what if you are looking at a stock and you expect that the price is going to decrease? When this situation occurs, you can choose to borrow shares and then later sell them with the expectation that you will purchase them back at a lower price and make a profit later on. At this point, you may be wondering how it is possible for you to sell shares that you don't own or that you don't hold in your own account?

This is pretty simple. Brokerages have a mechanism that will allow a trader to borrow the shares. When you end up selling shares that you don't actually own, it means that you are "going short" or "being short' on a stock. When a trader says that they are short on a stock, it means that they borrowed shares from the broker and then sold them with the expectations that the price will drop, and they will be able to replace those shares by purchasing them later at a lower price.

When you are setting up an account to trade, you will probably need to take the time to fill out some additional forms with the broker so that you can take this short position with a stock. You should also have an idea that this option can be riskier compared to just going long or purchasing a stock, so you must be actively there to manage the position.

Short selling can be an important tool for you as a swing trader because the prices of the stocks are usually going to drop much faster than they will go up. It is a good rule of thumb to say that stocks are going to fall three times faster than they rise. This is often because of the human psyche; the fear of loss is more powerful than the desire for a gain.

When the stock starts to move down, shareholders are going to fear that they will have to lose their profits or gains, and they move to sell that quickly. This selling activity is going to feed into more selling as shareholders continue to take the profits and traders start to shorten. This additional shorting activity adds to the downward pressure that is there on the price. This sends the price of the stock into a strong decline, which means that short sellers are able to make a good amount of profits while long traders and other investors are going to enter panic mode and may try to dump their shares to protect themselves.

Knowing this information can make it easier to do the trades that you want. It can help you to figure out which position you would like to enter based on how the market or that particular stock is doing at the time. This also shows you that it is possible to get into the market and make profits, no matter which direction you think the market is heading.

How to Enter a Trade

If you are brand new to trading, you are probably curious about how you would sell or purchase a security. Any time that the market is open, there are going to be two prices for any security that can be traded. There will be the bid price and the ask price. The bid price is what buying or purchasing traders are offering to pay for that stock right then. The ask price, on the other hand, is the price that traders want in order to sell that security.

You will quickly notice that the bid price is always going to be a bit lower simply because the buyers want to pay less, and the asking price is always going to be higher because sellers want more for their holdings. The difference between these two prices is known as the spread.

The spreads that are found will vary for each stock, and they can even change throughout the day. If a stock doesn't have a ton of buyers and sellers, then there could be a bigger spread. When there are more buyers and sellers, then the spread between these two prices will be much lower.

As a swing trader, when you are ready to enter into a position, you are going to have two choices. You can either go in or pay the price that the seller is asking for right away or you can place a bid that is at or below the bid price. Paying the asking price immediately can be beneficial because it ensures that the purchase transaction is completed or filled but may mean that you will pay more for it. When a trader places a bit at or below the current bid price, they may be able to make the purchase at a lower price. But, there is the risk that no seller will want to sell for the lower price, and the order may not get filled.

When you are ready to get started with a trade, you will simply need to pick out your trading platform, pick out a stock, and then decide whether you want to pay the asking price or wait and see if you can get it for the bid price. Then, you can enter into the trade and complete the rest of your strategy.

Investment and Margin Accounts

There are two types of accounts that you can choose to open in order to trade stocks. The two main options include the margin account and the investment account. With a margin account, you can borrow against the capital that you have placed in your account. The investment account, on the other hand, will allow you to buy up to the dollar value you hold in that account. You are not able to spend more than what you have put in that account at a time.

When you decide to open up a margin account, you may be able to borrow money from the investment or brokerage firm to help pay for some of your investment. This is a process that is known as buying on margin. This can provide you with some advantages of purchasing more shares that you would be able to afford if you just used the capital in your account, and it can help you leverage to get more profits with your money.

However, there is a catch with this one in the form of more risks. When you borrow the money to do your investments, there will come a point when you must pay the loan back. If you earn the profits that you think you will, it is easy to pay this back. But, if you lose out and make the wrong predictions, you are going to have to find other ways to pay the money back. Making investments with leverage can magnify the percentage losses on your money.

As a beginner, you should stick with a regular investment account. Trading on margin can increase the amount of risk that you are taking on in your trades. This may be tempting because it can increase your potential profits, but there is a lot more risk that comes with it as well. You will do much better going with an investment account instead. This way, you can just pull out the money that you are comfortable with rather than hoping that you make a good prediction in the beginning when you are learning.

Picking out a Broker

During this process, we also need to take some time to discuss picking out a broker. If you have already gotten into other forms of trading in the past, then you can simply work with the same broker that you already have. But, if you are getting into trading and this is the first one you have done before, then you will need to search to find the right broker for you.

There are many different brokers out there, and many of them can assist you with swing trading. The biggest thing that you will want to look at is the commissions and fees that each broker assesses against you. Since swing trading times are relatively short and you will enter into and out of trades within a few weeks at most with each trade, you want to make sure that the profits you make aren't eaten up by the commissions to your broker.

There are different methods that the broker can use to come up with their fees. Some will charge a fixed rate for the whole year. This often works well for long-term trades and probably won't be an option available to you since you will do more trades. The two options that you will most likely deal with include a fee for each trade or a fee based on how much profit you earn.

If you can, find a broker who will earn a fee based on your profits. This way, you are not charged a ton if you do a bunch of trades during that time. If you earn a good profit, you will have to pay a bit more because of the percentage. If you earn less on one of your trades, then you won't have to pay the broker as much as you did before.

Before you enter into any trade, make sure that you discuss the fees with your broker. They should be able to outline their fees and can discuss with you where your money will go when you work with them. This can help you to get a good idea of how much you will spend based on how much you earn, how many trades you decide to enter into, and more. Get the commissions and fees in writing, along with any other agreements that you and the broker and their firm agree to in order to protect you.

Picking out How Much You Want to Invest

Finally, before we move into talking about some of the different swing trading platforms that you can work with, we need to discuss some of the basics of about how much you are going to invest in your account.

First, talk with your brokerage firm and decide how much you need to put in to meet their requirements. Some brokerage firms will ask you to spend a certain amount or keep a certain amount in your accounts at all times in order to trade. If your chosen firm has that kind of requirement, then make sure that you put in at least that much. Putting in more is up to your discretion.

If there isn't a requirement for a minimum, it is best to start out by putting in an amount that you are comfortable losing. No one hopes to lose money on any of their trades. But, it does happen, especially when you are a beginner. Putting in just the amount that you would be willing to lose if something goes wrong can help to reduce the amount of risk that you are taking on.

Getting started with swing trading can be exciting. This is a fun type of trading that moves quickly and can help you to earn a good profit in a short amount of time but still doesn't require you to spend all day on the computer watching how the trade is going. By following some of the tips above, you will be all prepared to take on some of your first trades with this strategy.

Financial instruments for swing trading.

When it comes to trading on the stock market, financial instruments are the specific asset that you are trading each time you buy and sell new stocks. Financial instruments represent stocks, bonds, commodities, currencies, and any other valuable instrument that can be traded within a company. From the market perspective, there are five major financial instruments that you can trade: exchange-traded funds (ETFs), individual stocks, currencies, crypto-currencies, and options. We are going to discuss what each of these are in this chapter, and which you should consider trading as a beginner.

Even if you are only planning on becoming involved in one particular financial instrument, such as ETFs or options, it is important that you educate yourself on what the other forms of financial instruments are. This way, if and when you are ready to diversify your portfolio, you have a strong idea of what else you can get into trading and how it works. Furthermore, as you read through blogs and various news articles to keep up to date on the market, you are going to see these terms being used in plenty of scenarios. Knowing what you are reading about can help you educate yourself, further improving your ability to make educated decisions on your own trades.

Exchange-Traded Funds (ETFs)

Exchange-traded funds, or ETFs, are the most popular financial instrument to be traded amongst beginners. When you trade an ETF, rather than trading something specific such as an individual stock or a commodity, you are trading more of a financial basket which keeps several different financial instruments in it. Most ETFs are made up of individual stocks, commodities, bonds, or even a mixture of these particular financial instruments. The "basket" or ETF is then awarded an associated price that can easily be bought and sold. As the ETF is bought and sold, the price fluctuates, which means that ETF prices fluctuate more than virtually any other financial instrument on the market.

Some ETFs are US only, whereas others can be traded internationally. Before you get involved in buying and selling stocks with ETFs it is a good idea to do your research and get an idea of where yours can be bought and sold, as this will help you educate yourself on whether or not it is worth your investment.

Regarding ETFs, their fees are often quite a bit lower than any other financial instrument that you can trade. The commissions paid to your brokerage are going to be significantly lower than they would be if you bought each stock individually, which means that you are actually going to end up with more money in your pocket at the end of the day, too. I strongly recommend that when you start out with swing trading you start out with ETFs, as they are going to be the easiest for you to understand. This way, too, rather than having to research and follow various different individual stocks, you can simply follow one ETF.

Although ETFs are simple and continue to be the best trades that you can make, it is important to understand that there are some drawbacks to trading in them. One of the biggest drawbacks is that people tend to become complacent and trade exclusively in one form of stock or another, and never fully diversify their portfolio. In certain ETFs this is not necessarily so bad because the fund itself is diversified, but if you trade in something more specific such as commodities, this can massively reduce your diversification. As well, if you do choose to have your ETFs actively managed by a brokerage, it can cost more, so it is truly best to learn how to do it yourself. Spending money on a brokerage will only cut into your earnings unnecessarily.

Individual Stocks

When people get started investing in the stock market, what they often expect they are going to be investing in are individual stocks. Investing in individual stocks is not ideal for beginners because they are harder to track and their patterns are more volatile and less predictable than other stocks. With individual stocks, you really need to be able to gauge the likely success or growth of a company to be able to predict whether or not the valuation of your stocks is going to improve enough over time to make the trade worth it.

Many times, when individual people get invested in individual stocks they are doing so to diversify their portfolio, as well as to take the gamble at earning more from their investments. That is because, as with anything, the higher risk of individual stocks can also lead to a higher reward from stocks.

If you do decide to get involved in individual stocks, you should be prepared to pay higher brokerage fees, or to have to engage in far more trades on your own. You should also be prepared to follow the market much more closely as you are going to need to know exactly what is going on in your particular stock, so that you can buy and sell at the right times. If you are not following the market closely, you could find yourself missing out on massive amounts of profits in a relatively short amount of time. As a result, you can completely destroy your ability to earn any significant income from this particular trade method.

Beyond the additional fees and market research you are going to have to do, buying and selling individual stocks also requires a high amount of personal discipline as you are going to need to be able to avoid making emotional decisions in your trades. For many people, it can be challenging to hold on when the market drops greatly, as you may have an intense fear that it will never come back up for that particular stock. As a result, you could drastically short yourself on earnings due to emotional decisions, when in reality what you should have been doing was holding on and waiting for the market to balance out again. Unless you have a strong sense of personal discipline, a clear understanding of the market, experience with trading, and the willingness to invest more time and money into your trades, you should refrain from using individual stocks. These are better reserved for people who have already invested a healthy amount into other stocks, such as ETFs, and who are interested in playing around and taking larger risks with a smaller amount of their investable funds. This way, you are not at risk of losing everything due to a poor investment choice.

Trading Currencies

When it comes to trading currencies: it is exactly what you would expect. You buy currency and sell it. Trading currencies is actually largely what places a certain numerical value on each currency, and is directly responsible for the strengths and weaknesses in the values of different currencies. Typically, currencies that are commonly traded are worth far more, whereas those that are not traded nearly as often are not worth quite as much.

When it comes to trading currencies, the market is open 24 hours a day from Monday morning to Friday evening. They close for the weekends, but are otherwise open nonstop. A person that trades currencies trades in what is known as "lots," which suggests the amount or lot of currency that you are trading. 1,000 is a lot of $1,000 in the base currency, and is known as a "micro lot." Mini lots are 10,000 or $10,000 or your base currency, and standard lots are 100,000 or $100,000 of your base currency.

Unlike individual stocks, where you can buy and sell just one single stock, you trade currencies in what is known as pairs, meaning that you buy one currency and then sell another. If you choose to trade in currency, there are 18 commonly traded currencies that can be paired together to create your trades. While many other currencies exist, they are not traded on the market, which means that you cannot buy and sell them. Of the 18 currencies that you can buy and trade on the market, only 8 of them are incredibly popular to trade. Those 8 currencies include: the Canadian Dollar (CAD), the U.S. Dollar (USD), the British Pound (GBP), the Euro (EUR), the New Zealand Dollar (NZD), the Swiss Franc (CHF), the Japanese Yen (JPY), and the Australian Dollar (AUD). Although you can certainly trade with the other 10, most trades happen exclusively in these currencies, and you should stick with them too if you are going to get into currency trading.

Crypto Currencies

Crypto currencies were introduced back when Bitcoin became an official currency in 2009. Since then, countless crypto currencies have been made and are now available to be traded on the market. Regarding crypto currencies, there are two ways that you can begin trading: you can trade by owning stocks in the company itself, or you can trade by purchasing the actual currency. If you choose to own stocks in the company itself, you are actually engaging in individual stocks with a crypto currency company. If, however, you choose to actually purchase some of the crypto currency itself, you are then trading the currency.

If you choose to trade actual crypto currencies, you are going to be trading much in the same way that you do regular currencies. You will need to sell one currency in order to buy another, which means that you are always going to require a pair of currencies in order to make your trades. Generally, crypto currencies are traded on separate platforms from other types of trades as they are considered to be a more specialized currency and they are quite different in design and nature from typical currencies, or any commodity. While the crypto currency is still traded in Forex (the foreign exchange, or the most popular stock market out there,) the platform you will use to access Forex for this particular trade will be different as it will specialize in crypto currencies.

Options

Options are unlike any other type of trade, as they are made up of agreements that declare that you have the option to buy stock in something if you want to. Buying and selling options means that you are essentially locking in an agreement to have the option to buy something at a fixed price, at a later date in the future. If you choose to buy and sell options, then, you are not actually buying and selling stocks but instead you are buying and selling contracts that offer you the option to buy those stocks if you want to.

The biggest benefit of options is that you are not required to buy stock, therefore you are not required to take action if the stock market does not go the way you anticipated it would. However, if it does, then comes the predetermined date that was fixed in the agreement, or the option, you can go ahead and purchase stocks for the lower price that was agreed upon previously. This is a great opportunity to purchase stocks for lower than their current stock value, meaning that if you wanted to you could make an immediate profit by turning around and selling those stocks again at the higher valuation. Many investors use this as an opportunity to get started in a lower risk environment when it comes to making investments. It is a great chance for you to get involved in the market and start making some trades without throwing too much money around at once, allowing you to ultimately hedge yourself against a significant amount of risk.

Because of how they work, options are an excellent financial instrument for beginner traders to get started with. You can use options to help you get a feel for the market, while also creating the possibility to turn quick profits from your trades, which is a great way to get comfortable with trading and earn yourself some money in the meantime. As with ETFs, however, it is important that you do not get too complacent and that you continue to diversify, as not diversifying your investment strategy enough can leave you at risk of losing a lot of your capital.

When you get started in trading, there are various financial instruments that you can trade to earn your income. Financial instruments are the "things" that people are buying and selling on the stock market in order to earn an income, and without them there would be no market to trade on. For this reason, they are a crucial element of the entire experience and you need to know exactly what they are and how they work.

Altogether there are five significant financial instruments that you can invest with, including ETFs, individual stocks, currencies, crypto currencies, and options. Each of these are instruments that you can buy and sell on the market, hopefully earning you profits each time as long as you follow the right strategies, including buying low and selling high. Each of these financial instruments has their own set of benefits and disadvantages, and they also have their own set of strategies and skills that you need to hone in on, in order to be successful at trading them. For a beginner, the best financial instruments to get started with would be either ETFs or options. Both of these are generally easy to understand, lower costs to get started with, and tend to be lower risk as well. This means that while you learn how to follow the market, make trades, and manage your assets and risks, you are going to have an easier time.

Once you begin to feel more confident in everything that it takes to make a successful trade, you can begin moving on to currencies, crypto currencies, or even individual stocks. With that being said, these three trades should never be made without you taking the time to really understand what you are doing, and having enough excess capital to invest. Before you ever invest in the more risky trades, you should always have at least 40-50% of your assets invested into less risky trades. Putting too many of your assets into higher risks trades can result in significant and even devastating losses that are not worth the risk. Always trade smart to avoid completely destroying your financial portfolio and having to start from scratch.

CHAPTER 3:
TOOLS AND PLATFORMS FOR SWING TRADING.

Normally, foreign exchange involves selling and purchasing of different currencies across the world. The number of participants in this market is very large therefore the liquidity is very high. The most unique aspect of the forex trade is that individual traders can compete against large institutions such as hedge funds and commercial banks; all one needs to do is to select the right account and set it up.

There are different types of accounts but the traders have three main options namely mini accounts, standard accounts, and managed accounts. Each account has its own advantages and disadvantages. The type of account that one opts for depends on factors such as the size of initial capital, risk tolerance levels, and the hours one has to analyze the charts either daily or at different intervals.

Mini Trading Accounts

Simply put, a mini account is one that allows the trader to transact using mini lots. For most brokerage firms, one mini lot equals to 10,000 units. That is equal to 1/10 of a standard account. Brokerage firms offer mini lots to attract new traders who are still hesitant to trade with bigger accounts or those who do not have the investment funds required.

The advantages of Mini accounts include low risk, low capital required and flexibility. The trader can trade in increments of 10,000 units therefore if he or she is inexperienced, he or she does not have to worry about blowing through their account and capital. Experienced traders can use the mini accounts to test new strategies without excessive risk. A mini account can be opened with as little as $100, $250 or $500 and the leverage can go up to 400:1. A risk management plan is the key to successful trading and in the case of selecting lots; a trader can minimize the risk by buying a number of mini lots to minimize risk. Remember that one standard lot is equal to about 10 mini lots and diversification reduces risk.

The main disadvantage of mini accounts is low reward. A lower risk translates to a lower reward. A mini lot account can only produce $1 per pip movement if it is trading 10000 lots. In a standard account, one pip movement equals to $10.

A subset of the mini account is the micro account which is offered by some online broker. This account has very little risk and also very little reward. The trade is 1000 base currency units and one pip movement earns or loses 10 cents. These accounts are best suited for traders who have very little knowledge about forex trade and one can open using as little as 25 dollars.

Standard Trading Accounts

The standard trading accounts are the most common for traders especially the experienced ones. These accounts give a trader access to lots of currency worth 100,000 units each. This, however, does not mean that a trader has to put $100,000 in the account as capital so as to trade. The rules of leverage and margin mean that all a trader need is $1000 to have a margin account.

The main advantage of this account is the large reward that one might reap with the right strategy and predictions. One pip movement earns $ 10. Again, individuals who own such accounts get better services and perks because of the upfront capital invested in the account.

The disadvantages include high initial capital and potential for loss. The kind of capital required to set up a standard account can deter many traders from venturing in it. Again, the higher the risk, the higher the returns and the vice versa holds, A standard account trader has a higher risk of loss because if a lot falls with 100 pips, he or she loses $1000. Such loses can be devastating for beginner traders.

Managed Trading Accounts

Managed accounts are accounts where one puts in the capital but does not make the decisions to sell or buy. Such accounts are handled by account managers such as stockbrokers and stock managers. In this case, the traders set objectives for the managers (the expected returns, risk management) and the managers have to meet them.

Managed accounts are categorized into two major types namely Pooled funds and Individual accounts. In pooled funds, the money of different investors is put into an investment vehicle referred to as mutual fund and the profits generated are shared. The accounts are further classified by risk tolerance. If a trader is looking for higher returns, he or she may put his money in a high risk/reward account while those looking for long term steady income can invest in lower risk accounts. Under managed accounts, the individual accounts are managed by a broker each in its own capacity, unlike the pooled funds where the manager uses all the money together.

The main advantage of managed accounts is that one gets professional advice and guidance. An experienced professional forex account manager will be making the decisions and this is a benefit that one can use. Again, a trader gets to trade without having to spend hours analyzing the charts and watching for developments.

One disadvantage that deters traders from venturing into this account is the high price. One should be aware that the majority of managed accounts require one to put in at least $2000 in the pooled account and $10000 for the individual accounts. To add to this cost, the managers are entitled to a commission which is calculated monthly or yearly. The managed accounts are also very inflexible for the trader. If he or she sees an opportunity to trade, he or she will not be able to make a move but will rely on the manager to decide.

Note

It is advisable for a swing trader to use the demo accounts offered by brokers before investing in real money regardless of the account he or she opts to use. Demo accounts allow one to practice without risk and also to try out different strategies. One rule that every trader should apply is to never invest in a real account unless they are completely satisfied with it. One of the main differences between success and failure in forex exchange is the account selected.

Opening an Account

Forex exchange has been around for very many years and some say that it is as old as the invention of national currencies. Over the years, the market has grown so much so that it is the biggest market across the world. However, it has not been accessible to the public as easily as it is today. From the 1990s when the era of the internet begun, many retail forex brokers have established routes through which anyone can trade in currencies so long as they can access the internet and have some money. There is a lot of hype and information about forex trade on the internet but not everybody understands how to select and open an account.

Currently, opening a forex account has become as easy as opening a bank account or another type of brokerage account. Some of the typical requirements are a name, phone number, address, email, a password, account currency type, country of citizenship, date of birth, employment status, and tax id or Social security number. Opening an account may also require one to answer some financial questions such as their net worth, annual income, trading objectives, and trading experience. Before one starts to trade on the foreign exchange market, they should make some considerations to ensure that they have a positive, secure and successful experience.

The Right Broker

The first step to trading well is to find the right broker. The activities of forex exchange are decentralized and there are hardly any regulations. Because of the over the counter nature, traders are advised to identify a reliable broker. This involves conducting researches on the reputation of the broker; to identify if there is a history of irregular practices. One may also want to comprehensively understand the services offered by the particular broker before setting up an account. While some brokerages support basic and plain vanilla activities, others offer very sophisticated trading platforms. Some brokers will offer the trader analytical resources to support better decision making while others won't.

Again, a trader should assess the fees and commissions for different brokers. Majority of Brokers charge some fees for their services through the bid-ask spread and in many cases, it is not a large percentage. However, some brokerages have some other fees and commissions and they might be hidden from the trader. When one is considering the extra costs, he or she should check if it is worthwhile.

The Procedure

Opening a foreign exchange account is not hard but traders should have a few things to get started. The trader will have to provide some identification information such as name, phone number, country of origin et cetera. Besides, the trader will be required to state his or her trade intentions and their level of knowledge and experience in the trade. The steps of opening an account may vary depending on the brokerage firm but normally it involves:

- Accessing the website of the broker and study the accounts available. The accounts include small ones where the trader can trade with minimum capital such as mini accounts or the sophisticated accounts designed for experienced traders such as standard trading account.

- Completing an application form,

- Getting registered (user name and password) to

access the account.

- Log in to the client portal and arrange for a transfer of money from the bank to the forex account. These deposits can be done through credit or debit card, checks, or electronic transfers.

- Once the funds are transferred, the trader is ready to start trading. Before trading, the trader may review the recommendations made by the brokers or extra services offered such as simulator programs.

Online Trading

It refers to buying and selling stocks or other assets by the use of a broker's internet-based website or trading platform. Currencies, futures, options, ETFs, mutual funds, bonds, and stocks can all be traded online. It is called self-directed investing or e-trading.

As mentioned above, in a split of a second you can trade stocks and other financial instruments such as the Dollar or Euro, some commodities such as Gold or Oil as well as main market indices.

One more advantage of online trading is that the improvement in the rate of which trades can be implemented and settled, since there is no demand for paper-based files to be reproduced, registered and entered into a digital format. Once an investor opens a buy position on the internet, the trade is set in a database that assesses for the very best price by searching all of the marketplace trades that trade the inventory in the investor's currency. The market with the very best price fits the buyer with a vendor and sends the confirmation to the purchaser's agent and the seller's agent. All this process can be achieved within minutes of opening a trade, in comparison to making a telephone call that requires several confirmation steps before the representative can input the purchase.

It is all up to investors or stock traders to do their research about a broker before opening trading accounts with the business. Before an account is opened, the customer will be requested to complete a questionnaire about their investment and financial history to ascertain which sort of trading accounts is acceptable for the customer. On the flip side, an experienced trader who would love to execute various trading strategies will be provided with a margin account where he can purchase, brief, and compose securities such as shares, options, futures, and currencies.

Not all securities are all readily available to be traded on the internet, depending upon your broker. Some agents need you to call them to put a transaction on any shares trading on the pink sheets and choose stocks trading over-the-counter. Additionally, not all agents ease derivatives trading in currencies and commodities throughout their affiliate platforms. Because of this, it is necessary that the dealer knows what a broker offers before registering with the trading platform.

Most online trading classes are centered on instructing marketplace mechanisms and technical evaluation, while others might concentrate on more specific strategies or particular asset classes. Courses may offer a comprehensive summary of technical analysis in addition to other strategies designed for specific asset classes. They assist traders quickly reach a stage where they are comfortable creating approaches and executing trades.

Fundamental analysis.

Of the two most broadly perceived swing trading styles, swing exchanging and utilizing a purchase to hold venture system, swing exchanging is by a long shot the most appropriate style for alternatives. The purchase to hold procedure is not generally reasonable by any means, since choices are essentially momentary exchanging instruments. Most contracts lapse following a couple of months or shorter, and even the more extended term leaps typically terminate following one year. Accordingly, alternatives are the ideal device for swing exchanging.

Swing trading is much less exceptional than day exchanging and furthermore significantly less tedious. With day exchanging, you must be set up to spend the entire day checking the business sectors while trusting that the ideal time will enter and leave positions. The degrees of focus required can be extremely depleting, and it requires an unmistakable range of abilities to be fruitful utilizing this style. Swing exchanging, then again, is an ideal center ground for those that need to see a sensibly brisk profit for their cash yet do not have room schedule-wise to devote to purchasing and sell throughout the day, consistently.

It's an incredible style for those that are relative amateurs and those that hold down all day occupations or have other time responsibilities during the working day. It's conceivable to feature potential swings, enter the important position, and afterward simply check how your position is faring toward the finish of every day, or even every couple of days, before choosing whether or not to leave that position.

The nuts and bolts of this style are generally simple to get to grasps with, which is another valid justification for giving it a go. You do not have a colossal measure of information to begin with; you simply need to know how choices work and be set up to devote a sensible measure of time to searching for the correct chances. There are definitely dangers included, however this style to a great extent empowers you to go out on a limb that you are alright with despite everything it allows you to make some better than average benefits.

You can set stop misfortunes or use spreads so you are never in peril of losing more cash than you are alright with. You can really utilize spreads in an assortment of systems, some of which are especially valuable for swing exchanging when you are not for all time checking value changes in the market.

Guidance for Swing Trading Options

Arranging and investigating are significant for anybody hoping to utilize this style. You ought to be solid and steady and have a smart thought of precisely what sorts of examples and patterns you are searching for and what kind of exchanges you are going to make in some random circumstance. You do need there to be a sure measure of adaptability in the manner you exchange, yet it can have an unmistakable arrangement of targets and a characterized arrangement for how you will accomplish those objectives. The market can be eccentric so you should probably change in like manner. Anyway a strong arrangement in any event gives you a stage to work from.

It is a smart thought to set most extreme misfortunes on any position that you enter. It's improbable that you will get your expectations and conjectures right every time you enter a position, and some of the time the costs will move against you. You ought to dependably be set up to cut your misfortunes and escape a terrible position; it can and will occur and you simply need to ensure that your great exchanges exceed your awful exchanges.

Great expository abilities are valuable. You don't need to settle on choices as fast as though you were day exchanging so you have room schedule-wise to investigate circumstances and work out the best passage and leave purposes of a specific example or pattern that you distinguish. It's likewise imperative to be persistent. In the event that you can't locate a decent section point to exploit a value swing, at that point you need the control and tolerance to hold up until an open door presents itself. You don't should make exchanges each day if there are no reasonable ones to be made, and the way to progress is extremely about picking the correct chances and executing your exchanges at the opportune time.

Correspondingly, you ought to dependably have an objective benefit for a position, and close your position when you have made that benefit. Attempting to press additional benefit out of a vacant position can simply bring about losing your benefits. You can undoubtedly set your parameters for constraining misfortunes and securing benefits by utilizing stop orders, alternatives spreads, or a mix of the both.

Alternatives Brokers for Swing Trading Options

A standout amongst the most significant choices you have to make before beginning with this, or some other style, is which stock merchant would it be advisable for you to utilize? Utilizing an online intermediary is not as fundamental for swing exchanging for what it's worth for day exchanging, yet you could utilize a customary representative in the event that you needed. Be that as it may, there are as yet numerous points of interest to utilizing an online merchant; for instance they by and large offer less expensive charges and commissions which will enable you to put in your requests.

CHAPTER 4:
TECHNICAL ANALYSIS.

When it comes to swing trading, minimal stock charts, rather than "noise," encapsulate trends. Therefore, by diminishing noise (algorithmic trading, dividend yields, etc.) on longer periods, a swing chart would reveal a network-wide market sentiment through trend analysis. And there are several ways traders uncover trends using basic metrics and advanced technical indicators.

Simple Metrics

Simple metrics are usually based on the concept that price is a result of time. They also aim at finding the relationships between time dimensions to predict an equity's general trend.

Highs and Lows. Highs and lows are the upper and lower limits for an equity's price at a given timeframe. An equity's overall trend can be obtained by marking trend lines through a chart's highs and lows.

Price Channels. Crafting a price channel directly involves connecting the highs and lows in a chart. This is a dynamic process where stop-losses and take-profit points begin to move, within the idea that growing higher or lower limit points aid in informing trade decisions.

Pivots and Bars. Color coding is the usual way in discerning a trend's turning points when using a bar chart or regular candlestick. These color codes are determined via the Up &Down Days and the Inside & Outside Days. Pivots or bounce points are usually generated from where price creates a fresh trend. Alternating between the up and down days is one example of doing this.

Advanced Analysis

Relative Strength Indicator. Measuring the relative strength of an equity involves utilizing the highs and lows that are relative to a timeframe you're trading on. This calculation results in a number between 0 and 1. This resulting number then produces a line plot and obtains a cyclical pattern also known as an oscillator. The highs and lows involved in this plot tells you whether a certain equity is overpurchased or oversold.

Squeeze Momentum. This concept is derived from TTM Squeeze as originated by John Carter. This is an indicator that's used to measure volatility. Through this, traders can discern whether price is involved in a cycle of high or low volatility and can make predictions of upside or downside momentum in what's referred to as an explosive trend. Squeeze momentum is obtained through calculation of a combination of linear regression, standard deviation, and moving averages. These metrics emerge from the ability of a trader to lay bare simple trends.

The Reason Technical Analysis Works

Whatever market you're trading in - stocks, options, forex, etc. - you can expect that there will always be predictable chart patterns. These chart patterns are most prevalent within the cryptocurrency market, though. Perhaps it's the fact that there are a lot of beginner traders out there that this is the case.

Many people who do not trade would consider this as gambling, but if you come to think of it, trading doesn't rely on chance or luck like gambling does. Experienced traders understand that success in trading relies on group psychology since technical analysis is nothing more than an evaluation of trader psychology represented visually. In short, there is nothing magical about it. Technical analysis is pure math. Yes, it has some predictive nature in it, but even that is a result of patterns.

That said, technical analysis works because human beings are predictable creatures, and that predictability is magnified when humans work in a group setting. That is human nature, and relying on that is what makes traders successful.

Chart Patterns

Aside from chart styles, chart patterns are another thing traders should learn and master. Chart patterns are simply the formation of price on a chart that can be used to predict the future movement of prices. Technical analysis is based on the concept that history repeats itself, and this is confirmed by chart patterns showing that a particular price formation precedes a specific price movement. This is the reason chart patterns are categorized into either continuation patterns or reversal patterns. The former signals continuation in a trend, while the latter signals reversal of that trend.

Types of Continuation Chart Patterns

Wedges

A bullish wedge often forms during an uptrend, since price trades within converging trendlines. These trend lines mean that sellers are doing their best to push the price lower but aren't as lucky as the buyers are. At the end of the day, the buyers win as the price breaks through, signifying that there will be a continuation in the uptrend.

Flags

The flag pattern is quite similar to the wedge. The only difference is that the trend lines that form a flag pattern are parallel and not converging. This type of pattern can either be bearish or bullish. A bullish flag pattern is formed during an uptrend, showing parallel trend lines both above and below the price-action, forming a downslope. A bearish flag pattern, on the other hand, is almost the same as the bullish flag, but the difference is that it is formed in a downtrend and comes with an up slope. With this pattern, the price target is often measured as the "flag pole" height, from the top of the flag and either up to the highest point of a bearish flag and the lowest of a bullish flag.

Cup and Handle

This chart pattern is basically a Rounding Top, but with a "handle," which is an additional pullback. It gives the insight that sellers attempted to push the price lower mid-uptrend, but there's a change in the sentiment from seller to buyer. Meanwhile, the pullback here is the final attempt of sellers to take command. After the resistance line breaks out, the target price can be calculated as the pattern's height. This pattern also comes with an inverse, which appears during downtrends.

Rectangles

A rectangle pattern occurs as a confirmation that the underlying trend is supposed to continue. Depending on the trend, this pattern is usually divided into either bearish or bullish rectangles. The latter appears during an uptrend the moment the price passes into a congestion phase at a sideways trading. There's usually a high chance for the price to break out in the direction of the trend that precedes. The break of the rectangle's upper line is the trigger signal, with the price target as the pattern's height. The opposite applies for bearish rectangle, with the pattern forming whenever there's a persisting downtrend.

Triangles

Triangle patterns come in three types: symmetrical, ascending, and descending. There's very little difference between the appearance of these three types, although ascending triangles usually have flat upper trendlines, while descending triangles have flat flower trendlines. The most common the symmetrical trendline, forming both during an uptrend and a downtrend. Similar to a wedge pattern, it comes with converging trendlines, although the slope is neither pointing upward or downward. A lower trendline's breakout point in downtrends signifies that the downtrend is going to resume, while an upper trendline's breakout point in uptrends affirms the underlying uptrend. The target price is the triangle's height that's projected to the breakout point.

Types of Reversal Patterns

Double Top and Double Bottom

This chart pattern occurs during an uptrend and downtrend, respectively. A Double Top comes with two swing highs at a somewhat different price and signifies that buyers weren't successful at pushing the price higher and that a trend reversal is imminent. What signals a trigger for opening a sell position is the support line's break, with the distance from the top to the support line being the target price. A Double Bottom, on the other hand, comes with two swing lows, and signifies that sellers weren't able to move the price downward. In this pattern, it's the break of the resistance line that's the signal for the trigger, with the distance from the bottom to the resistance line being the target price.

Triple Top and Triple Bottom

This chart pattern is similar to the Double Top and Double Bottom pattern. The only difference with this pattern is that it consists of three swing highs and swing lows. And similar to the Double Top and Double Bottom formation, the break of support and the resistance lines are the trigger signals. For Triple Tops, the target prices are represented by the distance from the top to the support line, while for the Triple Bottoms, it's the distance from the bottom to the resistance line.

Rounding Top

Among all types of chart patterns, the Rounding Top takes a bit longer to form. It's a representation of a slow change of sentiment from bullish to bearish, where the price forms in a gradual manner as represented by a rounded top. The support line's break for this pattern is the trigger signal for a short position entry, with the price target being the distance between the top and the support line.

Rounding Bottom

This chart pattern is basically a Rounding Top that's flipped in a vertical manner. The rounded bottom indicates that there's been a gradual change in the price from the previous downtrend. There's no difference in the trigger signals from the Rounded Bottom pattern, both in terms of the resistance line and the price target.

Head and Shoulders

This type of chart pattern signifies that the underlying trend is going to change. It is made up of three swing highs, with the highest of the three being the middle swing high. After this occurs a lower high, indicating that buyers were unsuccessful in pulling the price higher. The head and shoulders pattern is so called due to its appearance like a Head with Shoulders to the left and the right. There's also a neckline that connects the shoulders, with a break-out below it signifying selling, with the distance from the top of the pattern to the neckline being the price target. The inverse pattern of the Head and Shoulders pattern is called an Inverse Head and Shoulders if it takes place during a downtrend.

CHAPTER 5:
CHARTING BASICS.

Types of Price Charts

Price charts presents the historical prices of financial markets or securities over a specific period of time in a graphical way. The three key elements of a price chart include historical prices, trading volumes, and time intervals. Technical analysts rely heavily on price charts that they're also referred to as chartists.

Technical analysis uses different types of price charts, the most popular of which include:

A. Line charts;

B. Bar charts;

C. Candlestick charts;

D. Renko charts;

E. HeikinAshi charts; and

F. Point-and-Figure charts.

Line Charts

This is the most basic kind of price chart used in technical analysis. It links together closing prices for a chosen period of time, e.g., daily, weekly, monthly, using a line. Because it gives a very general perspective of a market or security price's current and past directions, it's the most common type of chart used in reports and presentations. Traders who believe that the most important or the only relevant price for a period of time is the closing price tend to prefer this type of chart when it comes to using technical analysis, even if the information presented is limited to closing prices only.

Bar Charts

Another basic chart used by technical analysts but compared to line charts, this type of chart provides more price information about a security or a market. In particular, bar charts show historical open, high, low, and closing prices.

This type of price chart uses a series of "crosses," where the vertical lines present the price range for the period (highest and lowest) while the horizontal lines represent the opening (left line) and closing (right line) prices for the period. It's color-coded, too, i.e.:

1. If the closing price is higher than its opening, the line is green or black, which represents an increasing period; and

2. If the closing price is lower than its opening, the line is red, which represents a decreasing period.

Candlestick Charts

As the name suggests, this type of chart represents historical price information in the shape of a candle, i.e., a thick body that represents the opening and closing prices and "wicks" or "shadows" that protrude from above and below, which represent the highest and lowest prices for the period, respectively. When the body is color green or black, it means that its price closed at a higher level than its opening for that period. When the body is red, its price closed lower than the opening one.

Renko Charts

Renko charts a lot different than the first three we talked about in that it focuses only on price movements, to the exclusion of other information like time and trading volumes.

Renko charts use bricks to represent price movements and these bricks are colored white/green and red/black. Their placements are dependent on how their prices moved compared to the previous brick. When the price of the security concerned went up from the previous one, the brick's colored white/green. If it went down from the previous, the color is red/black.

New price "bricks" are created and placed in the chart only after meeting a specific volatility condition, which results in either a major advantage or disadvantage for investors and traders. The time period for each brick can be as short as minutes or as long as a day, depending on current market conditions.

Renko charts are very useful for traders who prefer simple ways of spotting support and resistance levels as it focuses only on price movements. On the other hand, such specificity can make it more challenging to estimate general investor sentiment about a security.

HeikinAshi

This type of chart traces its roots in Japan and is very comparable to candlestick trading charts in that the color of the body indicates a security's price movement for that period. This type of chart more clearly shows price trends through color-coding. When multiple green-colored candles follow each other with no lower shadows, the price is strongly trending upward. With continuous red-colored candles with no upper shadows or wicks, the price is strongly trending downward.

So, what is the difference between a candlestick price chart and a HeikinAshi one? The latter charts or plots average price moves compared to actual prices for candlestick charts. By virtue of using average price moves, HeikinAshi charts don't show exact opening and closing prices for a specific time frame.

Point and Figure Charts

This type of price chart is normally used by more sophisticated traders because it removes "noise" information by focusing only on meaningful price moves. A point-and-figure chart features columns of filtered price movements consisting of price boxes of

O's and X's.

Time isn't considered when plotting point-and-figure charts. When there's no change in the chart, it means there's no change in the price of a security. Because point-and-figure price charts simplify drawing of trend, support and resistance lines, they're very ideal for identifying trends and trend reversals.

Chart Patterns

One of the ways technical analysis signals trend continuations and reversals is through price chart patterns. To simply the term, it refers to a discernable formation of price movements that traders can identify using curves or trendlines.

There are two general types of chart patterns: continuation and reversal patterns. As the names suggest, continuation patterns indicate that a currently ongoing trend will continue while reversal patterns indicate its reversal.

Trendlines

Trendlines help traders identify support and resistance levels and are drawn by connecting successive troughs and peaks, respectively. Successively higher peaks and troughs (upward angled trendlines) indicate an upward trending or bullish market. On the other hand, successively lower peaks and troughs (downward angled trendlines) indicate a downward trending or bearish market. When the trendlines are relatively flat, i.e., successive peaks and trough levels are roughly the same or they move back and forth within a specific range for a specific period of time, the market is a sideways moving one or is in consolidation mode, which is basically trendless.

Continuation Patterns

Continuation patterns indicate a disruption or a pause of an ongoing trend. As price patterns form, it can be very hard or impossible to know whether the current trend will reverse or continue. This requires paying very close attention on the trendlines drawn for continuation patterns, particularly when prices break above or below such lines.

One assumption about continuation patterns is that price movements within such patterns tend to become wilder the longer the pattern persists. As a result, traders also believe that price movements after breaking out of continuation patterns also tend to be larger.

The following are some of the most common continuation patterns in technical analysis:

A. Pennants: These are drawn with two trendlines that will ultimately cross paths because they're moving in different directions. One the resistance line's moving downward while the support line's moving upward. Often times, trading volumes go down while the pennant pattern forms and spikes the moment prices break out of the pattern.

B. Flags/Wedges: These are drawn using two parallel running trendlines that either slope upward, downward, or sideways. Generally speaking, upward sloping flags are common in bearish markets while downward sloping flags are more common in bullish ones. In most cases, trading volume goes down while the flag is being formed then increases when prices break out of the formation.

C. Triangles: Because this pattern appears more frequently than the others, it's one of the most popular technical analysis price chart patterns. There are three kinds of triangle patterns, all of which can last as long as several months:

D. Symmetrical triangles, with two trendlines approaching one another, which signals a likely price breakout but not its direction;

E. Ascending triangles, with a flat resistance line and an upward sloping support line that suggests a likely upward price breakout; and

F. Descending triangles, with a flat support line and downward sloping resistance line that suggests a likely price breakdown.

The height of the vertical line to the left of a triangle pattern suggests the magnitude of impending price breakout or breakdown.

G. Cups and Handles: This is a bullish (upward trending)

continuation pattern. The cup-looking left part of the pattern resembles the shape of the letter U or a bowl, with both sides of said "cup" registering equal high prices. To the right of the "cup" is the handle, which is formed by a brief price pullback that looks more like a pennant or flag continuation pattern. After the handle is completed, the price of the security concerned will most likely breakout and reach new highs and continue its upward trend.

Reversal Patterns

As the name suggests, these are price chart patterns that signal the end of a trend and the start of a new one. This signals that one camp has run out of steam and the other camp has overcome them already until the beaten camp regains momentum and the winning camp eventually loses momentum and the trend is reversed.

Take for example a reversal in a previous bull market, where bullish traders outnumber and outpower bearish ones. When the bullish traders lose steam, the bears overpower them reverse the trend from a bullish to a bearish one, and continue to rule a market until they lose momentum themselves and the bulls regain it to reverse the trend again.

When reversals happen during market peaks, they're called distribution patterns. This indicates more traders are eager to sell than to buy, causing prices to reverse and start going down.

When reversals happen during market bottoms or troughs,

they're called accumulation patterns. It's because more traders are eager to buy or accumulate more of a particular security, which starts to push the price up and reverse the bearish trend.

Much like continuation patterns, the size of the price breakout at reversal is highly influenced by the length of time reversal patterns take to form. The longer it takes, the greater the price move upon breakout or reversal.

Some of the most common reversal price chart patterns include:

A. Head and Shoulders: This type of pattern appears as a series of three price pushes that include an initial peak (first shoulder), a second but higher peak (the head), and a third peak (second shoulder) that closely resembles the first one. A head and shoulders pattern occurs at the end of a bull market or trend, the completion of which signifies a reversal to a bearish market or trend.

B. Inverse Head and Shoulders: This pattern is formed by three major price movements as the head and shoulders, albeit in an opposite direction. It includes an initial trough (first inverted shoulder), a second but lower trough (the inverted head), and a third trough that approximates the first one (second inverted shoulder). This type of reversal pattern occurs towards the end of a bear market or trend, the completion of which signals a reversal to a bullish market or trend.

C. Double Tops and Bottoms: These patterns represent two

attempts at breaking through established resistance and support levels. A double top pattern resembles the letter M, where the price unsuccessfully tries to breach a specific resistance level during a bull market or bullish trend. These unsuccessful attempts often lead to a reversal, i.e., a bear market or trend.

A double bottom pattern happens during bear markets and resembles the letter W where prices fail to breach a specific support level. Such unsuccessful attempts result in a trend reversal to a bull market.

D. Triple Tops: This reversal pattern resembles that of the double tops/bottoms but with an extra top/bottom. Compared to double tops/bottoms and head and shoulders patterns, triple tops are unicorns in that they don't happen frequently.

E. Price Gaps: As the name suggests, gaps are empty spaces that lie between two particular time periods. Gaps form when the next period's security price has jumped or dropped considerably from the previous period. For example, the price of Stock A closed at $5.00 the day before and opened at $6.00 the next trading day, resulting in a $1.00 gap.

There are three kinds of price gaps: breakaway, runaway, and exhaustion gaps. The difference between the three lies in their timing.

Breakaway gaps occur at the start of a new trend. Runaway gaps occur in the middle and exhaustion gaps occur towards the end of an existing trend.

CHAPTER 6:
INDICATOR TOOLS

Technical indicators refer to mathematical models that strive to predict a security or market's future price movements using data such as historical prices, trading volume, and open interest. Some of the most popular technical indicators traders use to time their trades include the moving averages (MA), moving average convergence divergence (MACD), relative strength indicator (RSI), Money Flow Index (MFI), Stochastics, and Bollinger Bands. Best Indicators for Swing Traders

There are plenty of indicators that traders and investors use to enhance their trades. We shall review just a few of these and discover the best way of applying them to our trades in order to maximize profitability. It is crucial to understand that none of these indicators will make you profitable from the onset. Therefore, do not stress over trying to find the best or most profitable trade indicators. Instead, focus more on learning about a couple of extremely effective indicators as well as the strategies and methods used alongside them. Experts believe that trading strategies are more profitable when you apply the few indicators that you have mastered.

1. Moving Averages

Moving averages are among the most important trade indicators used by swing traders. They are defined as lines drawn across a chart and are determined based on previous prices. Moving averages are really to understand, yet they are absolutely useful when it comes to trading the markets. They are extremely useful to all kinds of traders, including swing traders, day traders, intra-day traders, and long-term investors.

You need to ensure that you have a number of moving averages plotted across your trading charts all with different time periods. For instance, you can have the 100-day moving average, the 50-day, and the 9-day MA. This way, you will obtain a much broader overview of the market and be able to identify much stronger reversals and trends.

Once you have plotted and drawn the moving averages on your charts, you can then use them for a number of purposes. The first is to identify the strength of a trend. Basically, what you need to do is to observe the lines and gauge their distance from the current stock price.

A trend is considered weak if the trend and the current price are far from the relative MA. The farther they are then, the weaker the trend is. This makes it easier for traders to note any possible reversals and also identify exit and entry points. You should use Moving Averages together with additional indicators—for instance, the volume.

Moving averages can also be used to identify trend reversals. When you plot multiple moving averages, they are bound to cross. If they do, then this implies a couple of things. For instance, crossing MA lines indicate a trend reversal. If these cross after an uptrend, then it means that the trend is about to change direction and a bearish one is about to appear.

However, some trend reversals are never real, so you have to be careful before calling out one. Many traders are often caught off guard by these false reversals. Therefore, confirm them before trading using other tools and methods. Even then, the moving average is a very vital indicator. They enable traders to get a true feel and understanding of the markets.

2. RSI – Relative Strength Index

Another crucial indicator that is commonly used by swing traders and other traders is the RSI or relative strength index. This index is also an indicator that evaluates the strength of the price of a security that you may be interested in. The figure indicated is relative and provides traders with a picture of how the stock is performing relative to the markets. You will need information regarding volatility and past performance. All traders, regardless of their trading styles, need this useful indicator. Using this relative evaluation tool gives you a figure that lies between 1 and 100.

Tips on RSI Use

The relative strength index is ideally used for identifying divergence. Divergence is used by traders to note trend reversals. We can say that divergence is a disagreement or difference between two points. There are bearish and bullish divergent signals. Very large and fast movements in the markets sometimes produce false signals. This is why it advisable to always use indicators together with other tools.

You can also use the RSI to identify oversold and overbought conditions. It is crucial that you are able to identify these conditions as you trade because you will easily identify corrections and reversals. Sometimes, securities are overbought at the markets—when this situation occurs, it means that there is a possible trend reversal, and usually the emerging trend is bearish. This is often a market correction. Basically, when a security is oversold, it signals a correction or bullish trend reversal. However, when it's overbought, it introduces a bearish trend reversal.

The theory aspect of this condition requires a ratio of 70:30. This translates to 70% overvalued or over purchased and 30% undervalued or oversold. However, in some cases, you might be safer going with a ratio of 80:20 just to prevent false breakouts.

3. Volume

When trading, the volume is a crucial indicator and constitutes a major part of any trading strategy. As a trader, you want to always target stocks with high volumes as these are considered liquid. How many traders, especially new ones, often disregard volume and look at other indicators instead.

While volume is great for liquidity purposes, it is also desirable for trend. A good trend should be supported by volume. A large part of any stock's volume should constitute part of any trend for it to be a true and reliable trend.

Most of the time traders will observe a trend based on price action. You need to also be on the lookout for new money which means additional players and volume. If you note significant volumes contributing to a trend, then you can be confident about your analysis. Even when it comes to a downtrend, there should be sufficient volumes visible for it to be considered trustworthy. A lack of volume simply means a stock has either been undervalued or overvalued.

4. Bollinger Bands Indicator

One of the most important indicators that you will need is the Bollinger band indicator. It is a technical indicator that performs two crucial purposes. The first is to identify sections of the market that are overbought and oversold. The other purpose is to check the market's volatility.

This indicator consists of 3 distinct moving averages. There is a central one which is an SMA or simple moving average and then there two on each side of the SMA. These are also moving averages but are plotted on either side of the central SMA about 2 standard deviations away. These bands can be clearly viewed in the diagram below.

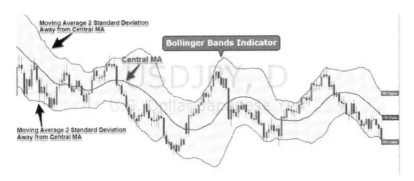

5. Accumulation and Distribution Line

Another indicator that is widely used by swing traders is the accumulation/distribution line. This indicator is generally used to track the money flow within a security. The money that flows into and out of a particular stock provides useful information for your analysis.

The accumulation/distribution indicator compares very well with another indicator, the OBV, or the on-balance volume indicator. The difference, in this case, is that it considers the trading range as well as the closing price of a stock. The OBV only considers the trading range for a given period.

When a security closes out close to its high, then the accumulation/distribution indicator will add weight to the stock value compared to closing out close to the mid-point. Depending on your needs and sometimes the calculations, you may also want to use the OBV indicator.

You can use this indicator to confirm an upward trend. For instance, when it is trending upwards, you will observe buying interest because the security will close at a point that is higher than the mid-range. However, when it closes at a point that is lower than the mid-range, then the volume is indicated as negative, and this indicates a declining trend.

While using this indicator, you will also want to be on the lookout for divergence. When the accumulation/distribution begins to decline while the price is going up, then you should be careful because this signals a possible reversal. On the other hand, if the trend starts to ascend while the price is falling, then this probably indicates a possible price rise in the near future. It is advisable to ensure that your internet and other connections are extremely fast, especially when using these indicators, as time is essential.

6. The Average Directional Index, ADX

Another tool or indicator that is widely used by swing traders is the average directional index, the ADX. This indicator is basically a trend indicator, and its purpose is largely to check the momentum and strength of a trend. A trend is believed to have directional strength if the ADX value is equal to or higher than

40. The directional could be upwards or downward based on the general price direction. However, when the ADX value is below 20, then we can say that there is no trend or there is one, but it is weak and unreliable.

7. Aroon Technical Indicator

Another useful indicator that you can use is the Aroon indicator. This is a technical indicator designed to check if a particular financial security is trending. It also checks to find out whether the security's price is achieving new lows or new highs over a given period of time.

You can also use this technical indicator to discover the onset of a new trend. It features two distinct lines, which are the "Aroon down" line and the "Aroon up" line. A trend is noted when the "Aroon up" line traverses across the "Aroon down" line. To confirm the trend, then the "Aroon up" line will get to 100-point mark and stay there.

The reverse holds water as well. When the "Aroon down" line cuts below the "Aroon up" line, then we can presume a downward trend. To confirm this, we should note the line that is getting close to the 100-point mark and staying there.

This popular trading tool comes with a calculator which you can use to determine a few things. If the trend is bullish or bearish, then the calculator will let you know. The formulas used to determine this refer to the most recent highs and lows. When the Aroon values are high, then recent values were used; when they are low, the values used were less recent. Typical Aroon values vary between 0 and 100. Figures that are close to 0 indicate a weak trend while those closer to 100 indicate a strong trend.

The bullish and bearish Aroon indicators can be converted into one oscillator. This is done by making the bearish one range from 0 to -100 while the bullish one ranges from 100 to 0. The combined indicator will then oscillate between 100 and -100. 100 will indicate a strong trend, 0 means there is no trend while -100 implies a negative or downward trend.

This trading tool is pretty easy to use. What you need to is first obtain the necessary figures then plot these on the relevant chart. When you then plot these figures on the chart, watch out for the two key levels. These are 30 and 70. Anything above the 70-point mark means the trend is solid while anything below 30 implies a weak trend.

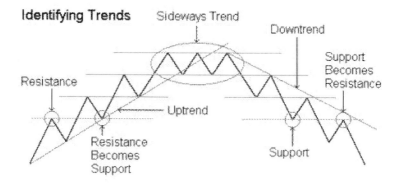

CHAPTER 7:
TREND

Okay, we've looked at stages and waves. Now let's turn our attention to trends.

To put it simply, a trend is the relatively consistent price movement in one predominant direction within a particular time frame. These price movements could be either sideways, up, or down so long as they are fairly consistent for a considerable amount of time. Trends may last for as long as several months; a huge profit-making period for traders who can see the bigger picture.

Countertrends

It is possible to have a countertrend within a predominant trend (the bigger picture). This is not just a pullback or a rally; it is period where a trend goes in the opposite direction of a major trend for as long as several weeks or months. However, its price movements eventually return to the major trend. This is good for you as a swing trader because you are not in the market for the long-haul. So you can make a profit from both the predominant trend (bigger picture) and from the countertrend.

Short-term Trends

Within the predominant trend, there is also the possibility of having short-term trends which are super cool for swing traders. Short-term trends can sometimes last for as long as several days to weeks. But guess what: short-term trends are usually not apparent when you are looking at the bigger picture – the predominant trend. You need to zoom in closer to see them. So, take a look at any stock chart that shows a predominant trend for several months, but this time, magnify the chart to show you daily trends. You can zoom in closer to see hourly or shorter time periods. There you will find swing trading honeypots that are of no interest to the buy-and-hold investor, but which are goldmines to the swing trader!

Trending Stocks

As a beginner, if you really want to make money from swing trading over and over again, you should trade trending stocks (stocks that are in an uptrend or downtrend). And here is how to know a trending stock. A stock in an uptrend has higher highs and higher lows. In other words, a stock in the second stage is in an upward trend. Also, a stock in a downtrend has lower highs and lower lows. That is to say; fourth stage stocks are in a downward trend.

Generally, stocks are either in a trending phase or they are in a trading ranges phase. It has been roughly estimated that stocks are in the trending phase for about 30 percent of the time. The rest of the time, they are in the trading ranges phase.

Now take a good look at another chart below to see if, as a beginner, you would prefer to trade during a trending ranges phase.

Ignorance is what makes people who are new to swing trading enter trades during the trading ranges phase. It is very risky because there is hardly a chance of predicting any trend up or down. Trading ranges usually occur during the first and third stages of a stock movement. Remember, we said that you should stay in cash (hold 'em) during these stages. One of the fastest ways to throw away your capital is to trade stocks when they are in the trading ranges phase.

A Note about "Buying Cheap"

When stocks are falling excessively (in a critical downtrend), a swing trader may be tempted to go long excessively (buy larger amounts of stock) because falling price means cheap stocks. I would recommend that you should be very careful when attempting to buy into such stocks. If you must buy, you should utilize stop orders. Let me briefly explain why.

You see, in the stock market, as well as with every other aspect of life, "cheap stocks" usually have a tendency of eventually becoming cheaper. It may not happen all of the time, but it does happen. However, there is a possibility of cheaper stocks to rebound. But it may take a long time for cheaper stocks to bounce back up; time which a swing trader does not have. In other words, if a swing trader rushes into "buying cheap" he or she may end up amassing cheap stocks that no one will be interested in buying back. I believe that is not your aim for venturing into swing trading, yes?

Bottom Line

Practice looking at charts and pinpointing whether they are in the trending or trade ranges phase. It is a huge mistake to go long or buy a stock that is heading in a downtrend simply because you notice a sudden upward price movement. If the stock is truly in a downtrend, then the sudden upward price movement is a rally that doesn't last. It usually quickly returns downward, and that is a great time to go short (sell). The opposite applies to an uptrend. Do not go short because you observe a pullback. It usually bounces back in a short while. The sudden downward price movement is an excellent time to go long (buy stocks) before the bounce back happens.

CHAPTER 8:
SWING TRADING GUIDING PRINCIPLES

A few years ago, popular trader Melvin Pasternak established what he called the 11 commandments of swing trading. Today, beginners are learning more about swing trading because of this information. While Pasternak usually discusses these commandments in his class, he shares them through his website. Like most traders, he wants to do what he can to help you reach your full potential.

1. You Need to Have Long Strengths and Short Weaknesses

The first commandment focuses on bear and bull markets. When you are in a bull market, you want to focus on longer trades because the market is strong. When you are in a bear market, you need to focus on shorter trades because the market is weaker.

2. The Direction of the Market and Your Trade Need to Align

When you are analyzing your potential stock's trend line, pay close attention to the direction it is going. If the trend line is moving upward, the conditions of the market should be moving upward. If the trend line is moving downward, the market's conditions should be doing the same.

3. Always Take a Look at Long-Term Charts

As a swing trader, you are not going to hold your stocks for a long time. At most, you will hold them for a couple of weeks. Because of this, traders believe they don't need to look at charts beyond a two-week mark. However, many experienced traders feel you need to pay attention to the trend line over the last few months, even if you are a day trader or scalper. Doing this will help you get the best idea of the trend line. Moreover, it is helpful for beginners as they will be able to learn more about trend lines with various stocks.

4. Don't Enter a Trade Near the End of the Day

While this isn't always possible, you want to do your best to make sure you don't enter a trade at the end of the day. Many people feel that once the stock market picks up between 2:00 and 3:00 in the afternoon, it's time to find a stock to trade in a few days. The fact is, the market is so busy an hour or so before it closes because people are trying to close out their stocks. Day traders need to ensure all their stocks are traded before they close out for the day or they acquire high overnight risk. Because stocks are being sold, their prices are going to decline. While this is a pull for many people as the stock's prices are lower, it doesn't mean that you will receive a higher profit. Allow the day traders to sell their stocks and focus on your end of the day activities.

5. Don't Jump from One Stock to the Other

Do your best to make sure you are consistent when it comes to your stocks. While you want diversification since this can increase your success rate, focusing on different types of stocks can be stressful for beginners. You need to learn about the stock market slowly. In fact, even if you have been a trader for a while and find yourself struggling, you can take a step back and become more consistent with your stocks. This often helps people who are losing money on their trades.

When you are consistent with your stocks, you find that you are using the same strategy. This will help you become a master of your strategy. From there, you will become a master of the stock market. Consistency will help you learn all the details within swing trading. Because you aren't focusing on different types of stocks and strategies, you will be able to learn how to analyze charts easily.

Stress is a factor that can come with the territory of swing trading. When you are inconsistent with your stocks, you can find yourself feeling stressed as you struggle to keep up with your stocks and strategies. With less stress, you will be able to think more clearly and keep your focus.

6. Have a Clear Plan and Follow It

As stated before, you will want to ensure you have a clear trading plan and that you follow it. This will take a lot of self-discipline, but this is necessary if you want to beat the market on swing trading stocks. Take your time to write down your plan before you officially enter the trade. As you go through your day, re-read your trading plan as this will keep it fresh in your mind. If you find yourself struggling to hold the stock or sell it, look at your plan and remind yourself of the best moment to trade your stock.

7. Use Both Fundamental and Technical Analysis

By now, you have a good understanding of fundamental and technical analysis. While people generally turn to one or the other, you should try to use both as a swing trader. The reason why both are important is that you hold your stocks for longer than a day.

8. Don't Forget About the Psychological Side of Swing Trading

There is a lot of psychology that goes into trading. First, you can use psychology to help you control your emotions so you can always make clear decisions as a trader. Second, psychology can help you keep the right mindset. The right mindset focuses on having confidence, self-worth, and the belief that you will succeed as a swing trader. These are factors that you can psychologically build-up through meditation, breathing exercises when you become anxious, or other mindset building strategies. While you don't need to learn the basics of psychology and how your mind works, you will want to have a general understanding. This will help you reach your full potential as a swing trader.

If you do find yourself struggling with the psychology of trading, you want to start focusing on the positives. You can do this by writing down what is positive in your life. For example, you might make a list of all the people you love and cherish and who feel the same way about you. You also want to ensure that you are getting enough sleep and eating healthily. Both of these factors can cause you to feel negative, which will start reflecting on your mindset.

9. Put the Odds in Your Favor

There will be times where you will ask yourself, "Can I make a profit off of this stock?" You will find yourself stumped as you continuously analyze the charts to try to find your answer. You know you need to do your best to limit the amount of risk you have, but sometimes you feel that this is keeping you from making a larger profit on a stock. You can be right about this. Sometimes traders do become so focused on limiting their risk as much as possible that they forget to put the odds in their favor.

If you feel that you can handle a stock, but the risk is higher than what you are used to, you can look at setting a target price. This will become part of your trading plan and will make the decision for you. Your target price will tell you when to buy and sell. It is important to remember to set a stop-loss price along with a target price. However, you want to ensure you follow your target price no matter what the stock market's conditions do.

10. Be in Harmony with Your Trends and Time Frames

In trading, there are three separate time frames:

1. The longest time frame - a year

2. The immediate time frame - three months

3. The shortest time frame - a month

The basis of this commandment is the further you look back on your stock's charts, the better idea you will get. This will help you know when you should enter and trade. If you look at the first couple of weeks and struggle to understand the trend line, go back a month. If you are still unsure, go back three months. While swing traders will rarely have to go back to the longest time frame, it is an option if you feel you need more guidance with the trend lines.

11. Don't Create Isolation

There are a lot of tools to use in the stock market world—put them to use. While consistency can be key, you never want to become so consistent that you are only using one tool or strategy the whole time. If you are a beginner, you might feel more comfortable doing this, and that is fine. Work with your broker to get comfortable using a variety of tools so you don't create isolation. After all, the more tools you use, whether it's a strategy, chart, and trend lines, the less risk you will have attached to your trade.

CHAPTER 9:
SWING TRADING RULES.

These are my general rules, which have evolved through experience and knowledge gained over the years. It is up to you to develop your own set of rules, which may include some or all of these.

The rules are based on 2 factors that I consider important in order for a trader to keep their capital and have a profitable business. These factors include the following:

- risk of holding a security
- over-the-counter stocks

Each of these factors is discussed in detail below.

Risks of Holding a Security

As a swing trader, under the right conditions you can see significant gains just by holding overnight or up to several weeks, which is what makes this type of trading attractive.

Earnings Reports

Even if a company reports good total revenue and profit numbers, there can still be some negative comments made on "**forward guidance**" for earnings that the market did not expect. One negative comment could easily send the price heading lower even if all of the other results were very good. This would be great if you were short the stock, but not good if you were long and hoping for a move higher after the report.

There are other ways to play earnings report events such as using **options** to limit risk and potential losses. Options strategies are more advanced and are not covered in this book.

Announcements about a Product or Service

Any positive or negative announcement about a product or service provided by the company has the potential to move the price significantly, either up or down. Pharmaceutical companies are a great example of this type of announcement. Events such as the results of a drug trial can cause a stock price to swing dramatically one way or the other depending on the outcome. If the results are negative - look out below – because small pharmaceutical companies have been known to lose 75% or more of their value overnight. If you happen to have a long position in the stock, you will have a substantial loss. Just like earnings reports, the problem with this situation is that the trader does not know which side to take prior to the announcement.

Other events, such as a product recall that would negatively impact your position, can also take you by surprise. Alternatively, you might be holding shares in a small company that wins a contract with a large company. Singular events like these are harder to predict and can be primarily managed by limiting how much of your portfolio is invested in any one position.

Secondary Offerings

Companies that need to raise money to sustain their operations while they develop a product or service often do secondary offerings. Announcements about an offering are usually done after normal trading hours and might come as a surprise to many holders of the stock. These offerings are often done when their stock price is moving higher, which would have led you to think you're "on a good roll" with your long position.

The amount of the gap down will depend on how far below the current market price of the stock the offering was completed at. For example, if a stock ends the trading day at $30.00 per share and the company announces a secondary offering at $23.00 that is probably going to be viewed by existing shareholders as very negative. Recent investors at around $30.00 are going to be really unhappy and selling will likely follow. If the secondary offering was done at $28.00 on the other hand, then that is not so bad because the new investors are paying much closer to the market price.

The offerings are not made public until they are completed and so there is no way to know when a company might do a secondary offering. This makes them hard to guard against as a swing trader. The best you can do is understand it is a risk and companies that burn a lot of cash with little current incoming revenue are the most susceptible to this risk.

Downgrades, Upgrades and Short Sellers Reports

Brokerage firms and analysts are constantly upgrading and downgrading companies and modifying their performance expectations. Some brokers have specialists that follow only one stock such as Apple. Other firms have specialists that research and report on a sector like semiconductors. A rating downgrade or upgrade by a brokerage research firm can cause a stock price to move one way or the other depending on the sentiment expressed in the report.

There are also a number of firms that specialize in looking for companies where they can make an argument that the business model is flawed or where there is the potential for fraud being committed. These firms focus on finding companies to short and then release their arguments as to why they feel the company is overvalued. I recommend you watch "The China Hustle" (which is available on Netflix at the time of writing) if you have any doubts about how fraud can happen relatively easily in our regulated markets.

These analysts will normally release their reports outside of normal market trading hours, therefore, unfortunately for a swing trader, it is impossible to see these reports coming. Like many other unique events, the only way to protect yourself from a big loss is to practice your risk to reward strategies and limit how much of your total portfolio is invested in one position.

Other Announcements

Any other negative announcement such as a data breach, an SEC investigation, or a new lawsuit can hurt your position if you're long. A positive announcement such as the introduction of a new product, a partnership with another company, or the resolution of a lawsuit can negatively impact your account if you are short.

Unanticipated events are one of the challenges a swing trader faces and, as with all other unexpected occurrences, the best way to protect yourself from these is to practice your risk to reward plan. There is always the possibility that a singular event will work in your favor, such as being long a stock that announces a major partnership. You are there to capture the upside but you need to follow your trading plan and your risk to reward plan to protect your account on the downside.

Changes in Market Sentiment

Events and announcements can change market sentiment overnight. Regular reports such as the Institute of Supply Management's Manufacturing Purchasing Managers' Index (known as the PMI) are used as an indicator of the overall economic condition of the manufacturing sector. A release of an unexpected number can cause the overall market sentiment to become more positive or negative. With the PMI, a reading above 50 indicates that that particular sector of the economy is expanding, and a reading below 50 indicates it is generally contracting.

There are numerous other government and non-government reports regularly released such as housing starts, non-farm payroll numbers, inflation numbers, and Federal Reserve announcements, and each has the ability to impact overall market sentiment. A swing trader should be aware of these coming events and whether or not the market participants are putting a lot of weight on the release of an upcoming number. These events are easily accessible on a variety of websites including Estimate (under its Calendar tab).

Over-the-Counter or Penny Stocks

Over-the-counter trading happens off of the regular exchanges like the NYSE, NASDAQ and NYSE American (formerly known as AMEX). These transactions happen between dealers and can include stocks, bonds, currencies and other financial instruments. The stocks traded can include both company shares that are listed on recognized exchanges like the NYSE and stocks that do not have a recognized listing on an exchange. These unlisted stocks are primarily referred to as over-the-counter (OTC) equities.

These unlisted equities are traded through dealers because they are too small to get a regular listing on a recognized exchange and therefore they are unlikely to meet an exchange's requirements for listing. Unlike listed companies that are required to make regular filings with the SEC, OTC equities may not file as often or with as much detail, which means there could be limited information available about the company.

OTC equities may also trade in just a small number of shares per day. This limited trading activity means that there is a greater potential for share price manipulation by insiders and that it could be difficult to exit a trade once you have a position.

I avoid trading any OTC equities for the reasons listed above. I also try to avoid trading penny stocks (stocks under $1.00 per share), as they can also be more easily manipulated by insiders and are therefore less predictable. On occasion, I may consider a stock trading under $1.00 if there is a strong case for going long, but it would be a rare exception to my rule.

There is no need for a Retail trader to trade listed stocks OTC. If a stock is not listed on a regular exchange, then I do not trade those equities. This leads us to my next rule:

Rule #5: avoid trading over-the-counter (OTC) equities or stocks trading for under $1.00.

CHAPTER 10:
SWING TRADING STRATEGIES.

You've probably been reading this book and wondering at what point we will start to talk about swing trading strategies. After all, you are probably most interested in the actual strategies that you can apply to make money swing trading. You can see though, that there is a lot to learn before you can start to understand the strategies that people use to swing trade. The market has many factors at play, and you need to understand the tools used to assess companies and their technical movements. You won't be able to use the same strategy in every situation, so knowing how to read the market is the first step before learning strategy.

The indicators that you are looking for will depend on the type of strategy you are using, so pay close attention to the fundamental characteristics of companies and you'll start to recognize similarities amongst different opportunities.

The first step is to make a habit of mining for opportunities. There are a lot of fascinating economic and business journals available on the internet that you can peruse for information about current events and finance news. You never know how you will identify your next opportunity. An article about energy companies in Texas may inspire you to research energy contracts in the American Southwest, and which companies to watch for. An article in a tech news magazine might send you on a hunt for publicly traded companies developing a certain type of computer hardware. If it intrigues you, then let yourself be drawn in for further research. The important thing is to spend a little time each day reading and identifying possible opportunities. Once you've noticed an opportunity, dig a little deeper and review the company's involved and check out their fundamentals. How have these companies been performing? Is it worth taking a position?

You can do this research by looking at the market sector by sector. Find indexes that represent different sectors you are interested in and check up with them every day. It's good to have a relatively broad field of interests from which you can identify options. One sector might be ripe with opportunities while another sector lags on the same day. Being able to switch gears and focus on the place where opportunities are happening will make you a more effective and well-rounded trader.

The type of strategy you use will also affect what characteristics you'll be looking for. If you are willing to take on a little more risk and you want to try swing trading, then you will be looking for stocks that show signs of a moving downwards. With the uptick rule, you will have to find stocks that are moving up now, but you have reason to believe that they will continue to drop in the future.

If you want to buy a stock and hang on to it and make a profit, then you'll be looking for stocks or sectors that are healthy and have continued and consistent growth. The earlier you enter a position, the better. Look out for signs of reversals as both a short seller and a bull trader. The sooner you enter a position after a true reversal, the more you can earn.

Remember the tenet of Dow Theory that states that the average of all the stocks in the index should confirm each other. You may just take a position on one or two stocks, but its good to have a picture of the entire sector. This will tell you whether you will be swimming upstream or downstream. It's OK to swim upstream as long as you feel like you have a compelling reason.

When you have identified a stock that balances risk and reward ratio, decide what price you'd like to buy-in. This will require some research into the fundamentals of a company so you can evaluate whether you are overpaying or underpaying.

One strategy that you can employ as a swing trader is known as gap trading. A gap is when there is a significant difference between the closing price of a stock today, and the opening price of that stock tomorrow. As a swing trader, you can try and take advantage of these gaps by anticipating that gap and choosing a favorable position. There are instances when the gap could go against you; like with a secondary offering or a bad financial report. But there are just as many instances when you can try to predict a gap.

Swing traders have an advantage over day traders because they can use this gap. Day traders are also less susceptible to the risk that the gap creates. Depending on your outlook and your strategy, you may see the gap as either a good thing or a bad thing. Unfortunately, with gap trading, you don't have much control if the stock price moves against your position. You just must wait for the market to open the next day in order to react.

Gaps could open in several ways. A company could release a statement of earnings, and as a result, the price of the stock could drop or go up significantly in a short amount of time. Unfortunately, it's hard to anticipate a company's earnings report in order to make an educated guess on a good position. Most investors consider it to be too risky to play the gap on an earnings report because it's too easy for there to be a surprise when the company releases its statement.

Another way to take advantage of a gap is by researching companies that are developing new technologies. This type of stock can be very volatile, with attitudes changing swiftly about the predicted success or failure of the product. The volatility could be an opportunity for the swing trader if they timed it right. Just be aware of the way the market can respond to an announcement about new technology. The stock price may shoot up to unprecedented levels as a result but often, things will settle down shortly after. Knowing how to time a position during a product announcement will be a major factor in whether you stand to make any money.

Remember; not all products succeed either. Sometimes a new product can hurt the company, in the long run, more than it helps them in the short run. Imagine an automotive company that announces the release of a new model. For a while, the model could increase anticipated earnings and investors might flock to the company. But the first model of the car might have more issues than expected, and the safety rating may be lower than normal. Remember that Dow Theory says that every action results in a reaction on the market. A product that performs poorly can do just as much harm as a product that performs well. Keep track of the progress of the companies in your portfolio, and make sure you time your positions well.

Another way a swing trader can ride a trend is to seek industries that are experiencing booms. Look for industries that are 'trendy'. Right now, the marijuana industry is experiencing a major boom and investors who recognized the possibilities of this trend early are enjoying a growing portfolio. With the legalization of Marijuana in Canada and many states in the US, there are new companies popping up all over as demand for the product is growing. Eventually, there could be a bubble once the expansion adjusts. But trends like these present opportunities for swing traders. Whether or not you decide to invest in the marijuana industry, its an example of a rideable trend. Who knows how it could play out?

These opportunities that exist in trends don't come around too often, and a swing trader must be patient in order to identify them. Usually, though, all one needs to do to find out about these trends is read the newspaper. Trends come and go and the window for making a real profit is limited. But if you're patient then there will always be another trend around the corner. The trick is to keep your ears to the wind so that you know when an opportunity has arrived.

Just like any swing trading strategy, a lot of it comes down to timing. A good example of a famous trend is the dotcom bubble in the 90s and early 2000s. A lot of people made big off the rise in internet technologies and computer companies. Eventually, though, the trend took a major dip and there were just as many losers from the dot-com trend as there were winners. Just remember that the stock market works in cycles and patterns, and these patterns often repeat themselves. Monitor your positions and stay up to date on news cycles.

When it comes to deciding on a position, timing is important. This means not only timing your exit but also timing your entry. It's better to be patient and wait for a good opportunity to buy when the stock price is low than to try and rush in out of impatience.

Before you open a position decide how much you are willing to pay. This is important because when you have a target price you can calculate exactly what you are risking before you even take on a position. Again, it's better to figure this out before you even take the position. Once you've determined an entry point then you must be patient. Wait for the price of the stock to match your ideal price. If it doesn't, then move on. Never forget that being a good trader requires discipline, which includes knowing when you should take an opportunity and when you should look at other options.

There are ways to track the price or set entry points without the need to constantly monitor the market. For example, a lot of brokerages offer alert services where you can receive notifications when the price of a stock has reached a predetermined target. You decide on an entry point and go about your day, then you receive a notification from your broker. You can even give them a limit order, which tells your broker to buy the stock for you once it hits that target. These notifications are also available for sale targets, so your broker can let you know when the stock has reached that target. They can even sell it automatically for you.

You've read about setting an exit point by now, and how sometimes you'd like to leave some flexibility in case the stock price continues to move in your favor. One way to do this is by not exiting your position all at once. Let's say you a buy a stock and the price of that stock has risen beyond your exit point and it is still moving. You want to preserve some of your earnings, but you are also curious about how high the stock might go. You take to exit your position with only a portion of your money while leaving the rest in. You slowly withdraw your position in increments, but you maintain some percentage of your position until you are completely ready to withdraw. This technique is called scaling out.

CHAPTER 11:

THE ROUTINE OF A SWING TRADING.

Swing traders differ from investors in various ways. Investors buy shares and hold on to them for lengthy periods of time. They often hope to generate annual returns, like 10% to 20% per annum on their investments. This is a different approach from traders who enter the markets and exit after a very short while. Traders hope to make small but frequent profits in the course of a few days or weeks. Their aim is to make between 10% - 15% or more each month. This translates into big returns over time.

Swing traders use both fundamental analysis and technical analysis to determine stocks with an upward trend and with momentum. A swing trader's work includes the identification of financial instruments such as stocks that have a well-defined trend.

The aim of a swing trader is to purchase securities when the prices are low, hold the securities for a couple of days, and then exit when the prices are high. This way, they exit trades profitably, and it is the method that they use to earn their profits. It makes sense to enter trades when prices are low and then sell when the prices go up.

As a retail trader, you may be at a disadvantage compared to professional traders. Professional traders are generally more experienced, have a lot of leverage, access to more information, and pay lower commissions. However, you do have some advantages in some instances because you are not limited to the risks that you can take, size of investment, and types of trades. As a retail swing trader, you need to ensure that you have all the knowledge necessary to take full advantage of the markets.

Trading Techniques

Swing trading techniques are easy to learn. They are also straightforward and simple to demonstrate. After learning these techniques, it is advisable to put them to practice for a couple of days until you get confident enough to trade live. If your practice trades were largely successful, then trading the real markets will also likely prove to be successful.

As a swing trader, you do not have to focus your energies using complicated formulas and learning complex techniques. You also do not need to buy and hold stocks or other financial instruments like currencies. Instead, you only need your trading charts.

Beginning of the Trading Day

As a swing trader, you need to be up early before the markets open. Most traders are awake by 6.00 in the morning and start preparing for their trading day. The few moments just before the opening of the markets are crucial as you get the feel of the market.

One of the first things that you need to focus on is finding a potential trade. You should spend your time finding securities that are on a sure trend. Another thing you should focus during these early morning moments is creating a watch list of stocks and securities. Also, check out all your other positions.

Current News and Developments

You should take time in the morning to catch up with the latest developments and news, especially those that directly impact businesses. One of the best sources of financial and business news is CNBC, which is a cable news channel. Another great source of market information is the website www.marketwatch.com. This is an informative website that provides the latest and most reliable market news.

As a swing trader, you need to be on the lookout for three things in the news. These are different sentiments in various market sectors, current news reports such as earnings reports, and the overall market outlook. Are there sectors that are in the news? Is the news considered good or bad? What significant thing is happening in other sectors? If something significant or of concern happens, then you are likely to come across it in the news.

Identifying Potential Trades

So how do you find trades that you'd be interested in? As a swing trader, you may want to find a catalyst. A fundamental catalyst will enable you to enter a trade with sufficient momentum. Then all you will need is technical analysis to confirm your exit and profit points.

1. Special Opportunities

There are different ways of entering the market. One of these is to find a great opportunity with so much potential. Great opportunities can be found through companies planning an IPO, those ready to file for bankruptcy, situations of takeovers, buyouts, insider buying, mergers, acquisitions, and restructuring. These and other similar events provide excellent trading opportunities, especially for swing traders.

To find these opportunities, you need to check out the SEC website or filings from companies. Certain forms such as 13-D and S-4 contain all the relevant information that you need. You can also subscribe to the website www.SECFilings.com so as to receive notifications whenever companies file reports. While these opportunities carry some inherent risks, the possible rewards are too great to ignore.

2. Sector or Industry Opportunities

Apart from the rare opportunities, we also have opportunities that are specific to a given sector. These are opportunities that you will find on certain websites regarding sectors whose performance is well above average. For instance, we can determine that sectors such as energy are doing exceptionally well by observing energy ETFs. There are certain sectors that pose a high risk but have high returns and can be very profitable.

3. Chart Breaks

We can also rely on chart breaks to find opportunity. Chart breaks are especially suitable for swing traders. Chart breaks are really stocks or securities that have been traded so heavily such that they are very close to major resistance or support levels. As a swing trader, you will search for opportunities out there by identifying patterns indicating breakdowns or breakouts.

These identifying patterns can be Gann or Fibonacci levels, Wolfe Waves, channels, and triangles. However, please note that these chart breaks are only useful when there is huge interest in the stock. This way, you can easily enter and exit trades. Therefore, whenever you note this chart breaks, you should also focus on factors such as price and volumes.

Securities Watch List

One of the things that you really should embark on is building a list of stocks or other securities to watch closely. The stocks that should constitute this list include those with a great chance at high volumes and upward price movement. It should also include stocks with a major catalyst.

Checking Your Current Positions

It is important to keep tabs on your current positions. You probably have other trades so take a look at these and see if there is anything needed on your part. This is something that you should focus on early before the trading day begins. You should review these positions with the benefit of foresight based on the information obtained from news sources and online sites. See if any news items will affect your current positions.

Checking this out is pretty easy and straight forward. All that you need to do is to enter the stock symbol into websites such as **www.news.google.com**. This will reveal plenty of essential information that you need to be successful. Should you come across any material information that can directly affect your trades, then consider what you should do, such as adjusting the different points like take profit and stop loss.

Market Hours

Now that the markets are open, it is time to get busy as a trader. During this time, you will mostly be trading and watching your screen. Check the market makers of the day and also be aware of any fake bids and asks.

Find a viable trade and apply all the skills and knowledge you have acquired to identify entry and exit points. There are plenty of techniques you can apply to arrive at these points. Think about Fibonacci extensions, for example. These can help you identify entry and exit points; you can also use price by volume and resistance levels.

As the trading day proceeds, you may need to make certain adjustments to your positions. These adjustments will depend on a number of factors. However, it is not advisable to adjust positions once you enter a trade, especially if you are planning on taking on additional risks. If you have to make adjustments, then it is better to focus more on adjusting the take profit points and stop loss levels.

After Hours

Most swing traders are largely inactive after the normal trading day is over. At this point in time, the market is not liquid at all and the available spread not suitable to enter any trades. Therefore, take this time to do some evaluation of your earlier trades and your positions. Examine your trades and see where you could do better. Focus on any open positions you may have and consider all material events that could have some effect on your positions.

Summary

To be an efficient trader, you need to have a routine. You should learn to wake up early before the beginning of the trading day and to get prepared. You also need to automate as many processes as possible. The crucial step is learning how to set up your workstation and your trading computer. Doing this ensures that you are totally ready for the trading day.

As a trader, you really need to learn how to separate charting from trading. There needs to be a different platform for charting, and in our case, **www.tradingview.com** comes highly recommended. It is just when you are ready to begin trading that you will log onto your trading platform.

There is a good reason for this. If you use the same platform for both charting and trading, you may fall into the trap of impulse decision. You will clearly view your orders right in front of your face. This will create a sense of panic and urgency, and you may do things in a hurry. When they are on different platforms, you create a thin layer that prevents impulsive action.

It is advisable to learn how to use templates a lot more effectively. This helps especially with the charting. Charting becomes an extremely effective and efficient process when you come up with different templates with varying colors. For instance, you can come up with a different color for resistance and support levels and other tools. The next time that you trade, it will be easy to track each tool individually based on its color code.

Also, remember to come with relevant alerts. Some traders prefer using multiple screens in order to monitor multiple developments at the same time. Instead of multiple screens, you can choose to create specific alerts so that should something relevant occur somewhere, then you will get to hear about it on time. Alerts are crucial and will ensure that you get to find out when there is a price movement and so on.

You can use the weekends to plan the coming trading week. You can do this without the worry or concern of active markets. You can also take the time to come up with different trading strategies and styles that can help you attain your trading goals.

Think up of different situations that can arise as you trade and then come up with suitable solutions for each. This way, should any situation happen in the course of the trading week then you will be well prepared to handle it. Sometimes, though, you may feel the need to use a trading template already designed. These can be found online and are easy to download. However, you can also come up with your own trading plan and strategy to implement. In brief, you should always enter a trade with a plan in hand. This means that you should plan your trade and then trade your plan.

CHAPTER 12:
A COMPARISON OF SWING TRADING, DAY TRADING AND POSITION TRADING

Swing trading vs. day trading.

Swing trading is very similar to day trading. The major difference is time. Swing traders last much longer in positions taken while day traders last on average only a couple of minutes. They exit their trades fairly quickly and never hold positions overnight. As such, they avoid exposure to overnight risks.

There are certain risks in holding positions overnight as swing traders do. For instance, major events could take place that could hurt a position. Also, positions can change overnight based on any of a number of factors. However, day traders are also exposed to certain risks. For instance, huge spreads between ask and bid as well as commissions can seriously eat into profits. This is a problem for swing traders as well but day traders have it much worse.

Also, there is a huge difference between day and swing traders when it comes to time commitment. Day traders are practically glued to their screens and cannot afford to multitask. A few moments' distractions and a trade could be lost. The amount of focus and dedication needed is extremely high. This is extremely different from what swing traders go through. Swing traders can enter a position then head out to attend to other activities. The difference here is that swing traders have a lot of latitudes and can head off to attend to other duties. Day traders are practically occupied with trading and cannot attend to other matters at the same time.

Swing Trading Vs. Position Trading

There is, of course, another style of trading that takes a much longer perspective on how long to hold a position. This is called position or trend trading as it is the one favored by hedge funds and large financial institutions. However, there is nothing to stop you from adopting a position style of trading.

The idea behind position trading is that the trader is entering the position for the long run. Typically, they will be buying a large amount of stock in the company as they seek longer-term profits.

This might be because they think the company is undervalued because it is underperforming due to market conditions or through a lack of financial investment or perhaps, they are just enthused by the company's product or business plan.

A good example of a position trader is Warren Buffett as he invests long term using his billions of dollars. However, moving that amount of investment is problematic as it would hugely distort the market value of any single company. As a result, institutions will often position trade by buying small batches of stock on a regular basis. This has the effect of keeping the target company's stock stable but does introduce all those little interruptions that are the bread and butter opportunities for the swing trader.

CHAPTER 13:
PSYCHOLOGICAL ANALYSIS.

Swing trading strategies, are very important for swing trading success. However, they're just account for half of your potential success. The other half is your swing trading psychology. Without it, even the best trading strategies in the world may not work for you. In this chapter, we'll take a look at some of the most important swing trading psychological practices you'll need to get down to pat to optimize your trading strategies' ability to give you meaningful profits.

Learn to Be Comfortable with Small Losses

As a swing trader, one of the toughest things you'll need to learn to live with are trading losses. No trader, even the best ones in the world, are immune to trading losses. It's a part of life.

However, many traders' emotions can get out of control when they lose trades, especially relatively big ones and when they activate their stop-loss limits then the security changes directions and eventually hits their price targets, making them regret their stop-loss actions. When this happens, many traders tend to let their emotions control their subsequent trades by trading with their emotions, micro-managing their trades, and losing objectivity.

You can minimize your risks for these by learning to take small hits or losses instead of bigger ones. This means a lower stop-loss limit, which is a good swing trading risk management practice. There are good reasons for this.

One is that small losses hurt much less. If they hurt much less, your risks for letting your emotions run your subsequent trades become lower.

Another good reason for learning to accept small losses is that you get to limit the size of your trading losses, particularly if your risk appetite's not that big. This means you get to preserve your trading capital much longer until you start getting the hang of swing trading and begin generating more swing trading profits than losses.

By learning to be comfortable with small losses, you get your skin in the game much longer.

Have a Long Term Perspective on Your Swing Trades

You can look at your swing trading efforts from a long-term perspective in two ways. First, you can set your expectations that it'll take you six months to a year to get the hang of it and start earning more trading profits than trading losses. That way, you won't begin and continue your initial swing trading efforts under pressure, which can make you make really bad swing trading decisions out of desperation.

Another way you can swing trade with a long-term perspective is to think in terms of your first 10, 20, 50, or even 100 swing trades! If you start day trading by focusing on the results of each and every trade, you just might make you go swing trading crazy and lead making foolish and impulsive swing trading decisions.

If you focus on every trade and evaluate your success based one trade at a time, even a small loss, which is expected, can lead you to conclude that your swing trading strategy's a fluke and make you jump from one strategy to another without really giving each strategy enough time and trades to master and validate. By jumping from one strategy to another after every loss or two, you'll never be able to master any swing trading strategy, ever.

Just like how your professors graded you in school based on the average of your multiple quizzes, exams, and recitations, you should also evaluate your swing trading success or shortcomings within the context of many swing trades.

Swing Trade According to Your Risk Appetite

There's no denying the fact that you can risk losing money by swing trading. Remember, the higher the expected return on your investments, the higher your financial risks. Because swing trading can give you potentially superior returns compared to bank deposits and other fixed income securities, the financial risks are also higher.

Many traders trade emotionally out of fear. Most of the time, the fear comes from the fact that they're not comfortable losing a certain amount of money. Maybe it's because their swing trading capital is an amount of money they'll need in the foreseeable future, which means they can't afford to lose some or all of it. Or maybe they're just not comfortable with losing a certain sum of money.

If you're like that, your best bet would be to limit your swing trading capital to an amount of money that you're comfortable losing, especially when you're just starting out. That way, you can minimize your risks for emotional trading, e.g., fear-driven trading, and optimize your chances of swing trading profitably.

Another important reason for trading based on your risk appetite is fiscal security. If you trade more than what you can afford to lose, you risk sacrificing your ability to meet some or most of your personal or family needs. The amount of money you should dedicate for swing trading must be that which, if lost entirely, will not have a significant impact on your personal or family finances. Never allocate your emergency fund or your kid's tuition fee money next year for swing trading today. Swing trade only your excess money.

Don't Be Greedy

Either way, emotional trading is foolish. On one end of the spectrum is fear-based trading. On the other end is being greedy.

When you're greedy, you'll always go for one-time-big-time profits and will not settle for small ones. The problem with this approach is that one-time-trading profits are very hard to accomplish and opportunities for such rarely come by. Greed can make you lose more trades than you win because even winning trades can eventually become losses when greed keeps you from exiting while ahead because prices eventually drop as you continue waiting for unreasonably higher profits.

This has happened to me before. I took a long position on stocks of a prominent real-estate company and after 2 weeks, I was up 30%. But I truly believed, or wanted to believe, that it could still go up and give me at least 50% return in less than a month.

On the third week, the price dropped such that I was still up but only by 20%. "No matter, it's just a correction and it'll resume its upward trend in a few days." I thought to myself. On the fourth week, I was only up by 10% and by the end of the fifth week, I was down 5%. All that time, I kept convincing myself "It's just a correction." I eventually had to liquidate at a loss of 15%. From gold to garbage – and it's all because of my greed.

Set modest swing trading gains and once your security's price hits your target, liquidate your position. At the very least, liquidate a good portion of it, say 50%. That way, you end up breaking even at worst if the price subsequently drops.

Take Smaller Positions

Another way by which you can keep swing trading greed in check is by taking smaller swing trading positions. How does it help you do that?

Setting unrealistic swing trading targets is just one way greed rears its ugly head. The other way it does is through large position sizes. This is because even if you set modest profit price targets, you can magnify your potential trading profits by going for large trading positions. For example, you can earn a trading profit of $1,000 through:

Profit per share of only $0.50 with a position size of 2,000 shares; or

Profit per share of $1.00 with a position size of 1,000 shares only.

You can double your potential trading profit by doubling your position size! However, you also risk twice the loss by doing so.

Just because you've allotted a swing trading amount within your risk appetite doesn't mean you should put it all in one security in hopes of raking in a windfall. Aside from setting modest profit price targets, keep your position sizes modest, too, by diversifying your swing trading capital across several securities in smaller position sizes.

CONCLUSION

With the information you've gained from this book, you are hopefully interested in starting your own account and beginning the process of researching your own trade opportunities. By now you have some foundation from which to do your research as well as a clearer picture of what to expect when choosing a broker and entering your first position.

The research required to be a successful swing trader won't stop when you finish reading this book. Every trade you enter will require another round of reading and studying so that you can choose a position with confidence. Remember what good research consists of; look at the fundamentals of a stock and the history of its performance over time.

Decide if you want to choose a strategy based on the stock or the other way around. Keep your efforts simple at first, take your time to learn how the market works. As you gain experience your trades will go smoother and you will learn what works and what doesn't. Keep a record of how your trades go. If you continue to swing trade, then over time you will participate in a lot of trades and hold a lot of positions. To learn from them effectively you have got to take notes ad keep track of your progress. You will learn faster if you keep a record.

The amazing thing about trading and competing in the stock market is the sheer number of opportunities available. At any given time, there are new profitable positions that are waiting to be discovered. If you genuinely enjoy reading about new companies and current events, then it will be easier to identify opportunities as they appear.

Remember that the best way to find opportunities is to research stocks and sectors that you already have a personal interest in. The knowledge you have already is a useful tool for staying ahead of the market. If you have an interest in cars, then you'll probably enjoy reading about automotive companies; what new car models are being introduced and how do you think they will perform? If you have an interest in computers and tech; what types of technology have you read about that you think could be groundbreaking? Out of all the new companies producing these technologies, which ones have the most promising fundamentals, and are more likely to succeed? If you approach to research this way, then you'll no doubt find opportunities for stocks to trade and invest with.

With all of this in mind, I hope that it is clear to you at least that swing trading is not a passive or easy way to make extra money. You must do your research. But if you find sectors that interest you, and you have a natural interest in current events and a keen eye for opportunities then you will be better equipped to succeed.

Take what you learned from this book and continue to build on it. Swing trading is a challenging prospect with many risks. But if you maintain a disciplined strategy it also has its rewards; better financial freedom, independent income, and the ability to control your own schedule to name a few. If you continue to learn then you are more likely to succeed in this ever-changing world of opportunities.

SWING

TRADING

STRATEGIES

A Beginners Guide Which Explains Step by Step Proven Strategies on Stocks, Forex, Options, Commodities and Money Management for Financial Freedom

Mark Make

INTRODUCTION

Looking for an experienced trader and help will not cut down your picture in any capacity if you want swing trading to be a constant source of income. It will just carry advancement and accomplishment to you. Mentorship is the procedure wherein a sound relationship is encouraged between an accomplished individual and a beginner for the improvement of the last mentioned. There are an excessive number of focal points of taking in the exchanging tips from a guide. Long haul objectives are acknowledged at a speedier pace with the assistance of a coach, spares time, more accentuation can be laid on the noteworthy parts of exchange. So as to receive the rewards of a coach, a great tutor must be searched for.

Significance of a Mentor

A guide will encourage you and prepare you for the rigors of swing trading. You will gain the particular expertise helpfully. Guides as a rule get the exchanging aptitude through experience. This suggests they have officially dedicated the exchanging botches the past. Looking for the help of a coach will help in maintaining a strategic distance from those blunders. Along these lines you can ace the craft of exchanging helpfully with no wastage of time.

Be A Fruitful Merchant with the Help of a Guide

As a novice merchant you will probably dodge those exchanging botches that are commonly dedicated. The complexities and the traps of forex exchanging can be gained from an individual who has just seen harsh and intense days in the exchanging vocation. This can change your rough method to accomplishment in exchanging into a smooth voyage of solace. Being a beginner merchant, having a tutor is required so as to abstain from exchanging botches. Coaches have effectively aced the exchanging methodology and can direct you through in your exchanging profession. Quality data on exchanging, exchanging courses are generally invited by the general population who need legitimate knowledge into the complexities of exchanging.

Characteristics of a Mentor

The most significant advance is to search for a decent guide who has the fundamentals of a good tutor. He ought to be believable, experienced, trying to do he really says others should do, offers unending help. A tutor should be trustworthy on whom the individual can depend. He should be receptive and agreeable too. On the off chance that you are looking for a tutor search for such an individual who encourages you in picking up trust in certainty is the way to progress. He should show you how to have confidence in the exchanging procedure that he/she is lecturing. Your tutor ought to be a present broker and not an individual who has left exchanging quite a while back. The tutor ought to have for all intents and purposes no issues over talking about an exchange over email. He should almost certainly answer your specific exchange arrangements.

A coach is a companion, savant, educator and a guide of yours. He should be very much furnished with the data available and must refresh you with customary market analysis.

Discover the Swing Trading Style

Maintaining a strategic distance from Psychological Traps That Ruin Your Trading

Getting rid of your own mental snares can just build up you as an effective broker. Forex instruction can be overwhelming. They are the hotspots for profiting and need practical parameters. The forex training or the substance on business sectors that are shabby, implied for being talked. There is a conviction that the market is irregular and no investigation can control the market.

The market is not irregular

The conviction on the arbitrariness of the market is senseless. It is a fantasy that the market is arbitrary. When you cannot foresee the market, you will in general accuse it by calling it arbitrary. In the event that we play out the Brownian Motion Experiment, which expresses that on knowing the speed, position alongside the mass can enable you to identify the rightest position of the particles. The definite position and the planning of the development of the particles can be anticipated with this.

This remains constant even with the forex advertise. In the budgetary market, the value developments happen when and benefit of purchasing and selling exchanges. On the off chance that you can pass judgment on the thought processes of members of the market, at that point you can foresee each move of the market. Markets are not under any condition irregular rather it is constrained by the purchasers and merchants. Like a horde it gives off an impression of being irregular on time spans which are littler since you cannot appropriately foresee the developments of the market.

A specialized examination when the market is on the littler time allotment will just give you factual edge. You can beat the market on the off chance that you comprehend the details that standard the market. It is anything but difficult to beat the theoretical market with the assistance of methodologies that aides in stopping the failures and enabling the triumphant dealers to work easily. Returns through the theoretical market are similarly more. It is just a legend that the market is irregular.

Absence of confidence: reason for dread among merchants

Dealers fear exchanging feeling that the market is arbitrary, however it is not the market, which is irregular rather it is the merchant's outlook that welcomes undue dread. Mental issues can make you believe that the market is arbitrary. On the off chance that you don't have faith in yourself as a broker and fear the business sectors the better take a secondary lounge and quit exchanging.

The best approach to self conviction.

On the off chance that you need to quit imagining that the market is arbitrary and cannot be tested then you are incorrect. You can challenge the market both authentically and profoundly. So as to beat the market truthfully outline a key inclining the more drawn out time periods alongside utilizing the shorter time allotment when you enter. You should for this situation, hold positions till the difference in pattern of the more drawn out time span happens, though you should utilize a tight stop misfortune on the underlying passages. Exchange the instruments that show ground-breaking patterns. Continue testing this for quite a while and in the event that you have sensibly assembled the system with no over bending fitted, at that point things can turn to support you.

Conquering the dread of the market is fundamental for fruitful exchanging. In the event that you fear the market, ask yourself the purpose for it and attempt to unravel it. Increasing poise without anyone else's input conviction and compelling exchanging can affirm you a decent merchant.

CHAPTER 1:
FINANCIAL INSTRUMENTS FOR SWING TRADING

Swing trading is tied in with searching for momentary value force and attempting to benefit from that value energy by purchasing and selling fittingly. As the estimation of alternatives contracts is to a great extent dependent on the benefit of basic protections, you are basically hoping to recognize the value energy of any money related instrument, for example, stocks, and after that exchange the important choices contracts as indicated by how you anticipate that the basic security should move.

There are really two unique types of swing exchanging choices: mechanical and optional. Mechanical swing exchanging includes following an inflexible arrangement of principles to decide fixed section focuses and leave focuses, and you can even utilize programming to figure out what exchanges you ought to make and when. Optional swing exchanging depends without anyone else judgment and examination to decide.

By and large you will enter a position and afterward leaving it a brief timeframe later. That timeframe can be anyplace between several days or half a month, contingent upon to what extent you are anticipating that the value energy should last.

With this style, you are not as worried about the key estimation of the protections included and how they will perform in the long haul as you would utilize a purchase and hold speculation system. While some basic investigation of the protections can absolutely be valuable, you are essentially hoping to recognize circumstances where a specific security is probably going to move sensibly altogether in cost over a moderately brief timeframe. This depends on examples and patterns. When you have distinguished that circumstance then you would then be able to purchase or sell in like manner with a view to benefitting from the value developments.

Swing trading should be possible utilizing most kinds of choices, and you can utilize various requests to take long positions or short positions on explicit contracts. You can even utilize a mix of various contracts and requests to make spreads which can incredibly expand the quantity of chances for benefitting. Spreads can likewise be utilized to restrict hazard presentation on a specific position by limiting potential misfortunes.

Swing Trading Options; Pros and Cons

Swing trading options are gets that give the carrier the right, yet not the commitment, to either purchase or sell a measure of some basic resource at a pre-decided cost at or before the agreement lapses. Options can be obtained like most other resource classes with financier venture accounts.

Options are amazing in light of the fact that they can upgrade a person's portfolio. They do this through included pay, assurance, and even influence. Contingent upon the circumstance, there is normally an alternative situation fitting for a financial specialist's objective. A prominent model would utilize choices as a successful fence against a declining securities exchange to restrict drawback misfortunes. Alternatives can likewise be utilized to create repeating pay. Moreover, they are regularly utilized for theoretical purposes, for example, betting on the bearing of a stock.

There is nothing free with stocks and bonds and options are the same. They include certain dangers that the financial specialist must know about before making an exchange.

Swing Trading Stocks; Pros and Cons

A stock or share, otherwise called an organization's value is a budgetary instrument that speaks to possession in an organization or company and speaks to a proportionate case on its benefits (what it claims) and income (what it creates in benefits).

Stock proprietorship suggests that the investor claims a cut of the organization equivalent to the quantity of offers held as an extent of the organization's absolute exceptional offers.

- A trade posting means prepared liquidity for offers held by the organization's investors.

- It empowers the organization to raise extra assets by

issuing more offers.

- Having traded on an open market offers makes it simpler to set up investment opportunities designs that are important to pull in capable representatives.

- Recorded organizations have more prominent perceivability in the commercial center; expert inclusion and request from institutional financial specialists can drive up the offer cost.

- Recorded offers can be utilized as money by the organization to make acquisitions in which part or the majority of the thought is paid in stock.

These advantages imply that most enormous organizations are open instead of private; exceptionally huge privately owned businesses, for example, sustenance and horticulture mammoth Cargill, mechanical combination Koch Industries, and DIY furniture retailer Ikea are the exemption as opposed to the standard.

Issues of Stock Exchange Listing

Yet, there are a few downsides to being recorded on a stock trade, for example,

- Critical expenses related with posting on a trade, for example, posting charges and greater expenses related with consistence and detailing.

- Oppressive guidelines, which may contract an

organization's capacity to work together.

- The momentary focal point of most speculators, which powers organizations to attempt to beat their quarterly profit assesses as opposed to adopting a long haul strategy to their corporate methodology.

While this deferred posting may mostly be inferable from the downsides recorded over, the primary reason could be that well-overseen new companies with a convincing business recommendation approach remarkable measures of capital from sovereign riches reserves, private value, and financial speculators. Such access to apparently boundless measures of capital would make an IPO and trade posting significantly less of a problem that needs to be addressed for a startup.

Swing Trading Crypto; Pros and Cons

You have some cash that you need to contribute. How are you going to go about it? The entryways which interface our reality to the crypto-universes are designated trades. There are a ton of trades out there, nonetheless, before you put resources into one, there are sure things you have to pay special mind to. The following highlights some of the cons and pros of swing trading crypto:

Security: Please dependably pick trades which need a type of ID confirmation from you. Despite the fact that they may require some serious energy, they are effectively multiple times more protected and secure than unknown trades. Toward the day's end, it is your well deserved cash. You should make that additional move to keep it secure.

Legitimacy: Before you even do anything, first ensure that the trade is accessible in your general vicinity. For example, Coinbase, one of the biggest trades but is not accessible in some countries around the world. So before you do anything please check this.

Trade Rates: Up next we have the trade rates. Various trades have their own trade rates which may fluctuate. Get your work done here and look into two or three trades and their rates.

Notoriety: Next thing that you have to check is the notoriety of the trade. Are individuals content with their administrations? Has it been hacked as of late? How secure is it? Have individuals grumbled about it? Social media and the internet in general are great hotspots for checking this.

Swing Trading Forex; Pros and Cons

A standout amongst the most important techniques for exchanging the Forex markets is additionally one of the easiest; understanding key obstruction and bolster levels in the market you have picked. Since monetary forms move in generally stable augmentations outside of significant occasions, when they start to achieve notable levels, either to the upside or drawback, it can give dealers delay for idea.

So, what are opposition and bolster levels and how might they help your Forex exchanging?

A help level is basically the descending cost at which a money will interruption or stop its decay as interest or exchanging volume starts to increment once more. Then again, obstruction levels demonstrate a high value level at which the market starts to accept a money might be exaggerated and it could be a solid marker of a potential auction sooner rather than later.

Both help and opposition levels are valuable as a major aspect of your general Forex exchanging technique understanding potential market section and leave focuses.

To enable you to distinguish key help and opposition levels in your picked FX advertise, we have various instruments for you to utilize. You can exploit our pointers like MACD, RSI and Bollinger Bands, include your own markers or utilize our attracting apparatuses to characterize key market levels you would like to screen.

What's more, you may think that it is helpful to set up a customizable Forex watch list with the goal that you can follow various value changes over the FX sets that most intrigue you or that could affect your exchanging technique. Or maybe, you are exchanging on value developments inside the fundamental market.

CHAPTER 2:
OPTIONS AND FOREX SWING TRADING

Options and forex swing trading are two types of trading strategies that are often overlooked. Options are when you create an agreement. Through this agreement, the options buyer has the right to buy and sell once the stock hits a certain price. It doesn't matter when this happens, as soon as the stock gets to the set price, the steps are taken to complete the agreement. Forex is often overlooked because it focuses on currencies. This means that you have to have pairs in order to make a trade. For example, you would pair the American dollar with the Canadian dollar.

Options Swing Trading

When you use options trading as your strategy, you are using the options market. The types of financial instruments, typically called options, which are used in this market are ETFs and bonds. Options are not run on the stock market because they are not considered stocks. While there is still risk involved, it does decrease because you are able to stop the agreement you set at any time. There is nothing in the options market that states you need to follow through with the agreement.

There are two main types of options:

1. A Call option is an agreement allowing you to buy shares at a later time and date. This information is often written into the agreement.

2. A Put option is an agreement allowing you to sell shares at a later time and date. Like the call option, this information is typically included in the agreement.

Many times, the agreed-upon time and date are known as the expiration date. This means that from the moment of the agreement to the expiration time, a trader can decide to buy or sell the specified option.

Like with other types of markets, there is different language associated with options trading. While you can use many of the same types of strategies as swing trading, you will want to ensure you understand the language.

You know you will enjoy options trading if you are interested in statistics and calculations as options trading is completely about calculated risk. With this in mind, there are two types of volatility you have to be aware of:

1. Implied volatility is when you are looking at what the market stated the volatility will look like in the future. This is what you base your decision on when making an agreement.

2. Historical volatility is when you look at the price fluctuations of your financial instrument throughout a

whole year. This means you will look month-to-month, week-to-week, and day-to-day.

Forex Swing Trading

Before you get into forex swing trading, you want to take time to study some of the most popular currency pairs, such as the Euro and American dollar (EUR/USD) and the American dollar and Canadian dollar (USD/CAD). What this means is you will sell one pair while you are buying another. It's similar to how you convert your country's money to a different country's currency when on vacation.

When it comes to forex pairs, there are four categories you need to be aware of.

1. Minor pairs are traded, but not often. Most of these pairs do not include the American dollar. For example, they might include Japan and China's currency against each other.

2. Major pairs are the currencies that are traded often. These pairs typically include the American dollar and make up around 80% of all forex trades ("What is forex and how does it work?", n.d.).

3. Regional pairs are strictly classified by regions.

4. Exotics pair a smaller currency against a major currency.

Along with these categories, there are three types of forex markets:

1. Forward forex market is an agreement to buy or sell currency at a specific price. This agreement typically includes the date or a range of dates that this trade can take place.

2. Spot forex market is when you make the trade on the spot. This is one of the most common forex markets.

3. Futures forex market is similar to the forex market but is an exchange-traded contract. This market focuses on a certain date and price for an exchange.

One of the nice parts about forex swing trading is you don't have to have a certain amount of money. There are a few strategies that will work with less than $1,000. Of course, you can use the same guidelines as you would with larger amounts of money. For example, you can put only 1% into your trade.

Because forex is a different market, there are different basics you need to know. For example, there are pips in the forex market. The pip's value depends on the size of the trade.

Forex is a bit different from the stock market because it is run on a global scale. This means it is typically open, at least Monday through Friday. Instead of remaining open from around 9:30 A.M. to 4:00 P.M., the forex market opens on Monday morning and then closes on Friday afternoon. This means it is open 24 hours a day throughout the week.

This doesn't mean that you need to pay attention to the market 24 hours a day, 5 days a week if you want to be a forex trader. But it does mean that you can choose to trade overnight, during the day, or mix it up. For example, you can follow the typical day schedule like a stock swing trader would do or you can start trading at 5:00 P.M. and stop trading around 11:00 P.M. Even though the forex market is open overnight doesn't mean there isn't overnight risk. The risk comes with your schedule. What this means is whenever you have financial instruments, such as currencies or stocks, in your portfolio and you are not watching the market, you are running a risk. Of course, this doesn't mean you always need to keep your eye on the market. But you also don't want to allow your trades to sit for a long period of time without ensuring your companies are still doing well.

Profit and Loss Levels

Stop Loss and Take Profit levels are your exit points in the market. These are the levels which determine how much of a loss you take or how much money you make on the individual trade. Unfortunately, the way most traders trade, they tend to morph these levels into Take Loss and Stop Profit levels.

Understanding the technical and mental side of these levels is essential to your performance, which is why we went over risk management and mindset prior to this, despite SL and TP being a technical subject. These levels are a snapshot of how trading works. Technical analysis combining with your mindset and risk management skill to ensure success. Let's take a deeper look at them.

Stop Loss Levels

As the name suggests, the stop loss level is that point on a chart beyond which you do not wish to be involved in the trade and would rather exit at a loss. Practically speaking, when you designate a stop loss level, your broker places an order at that level for you which closes your position for a predetermined loss.

So, in a long trade, your stop loss would be below your entry point. The stop loss order would be a sell order which closes your long position at a loss. In a short trade, your SL is above your entry point and the SL order is a buy order which closes your trade for a loss.

Most trading platforms provide easy options for you to place this order and it is essential that you do so. Beginners often fall into the trap of placing "mental" SLs because they feel their stops will be hunted by more experienced players. There is this erroneous belief that the bigger traders in the market push prices to a level where obvious stop losses ought to be, trigger those stop losses and then push the price back in the direction of a profit.

A Gnat on an Elephant

Let's get something straight. You as a retail trader are as relevant to the full-time professional trader as the events unfolding in

Antarctica right now are for your breakfast tomorrow morning. Yes, there might be some sort of a butterfly effect thing that might happen, but the possibility is a remote one. This ridiculous belief that institutional and professional traders wake up every morning and using their multimillion-dollar infrastructure go looking to make money of the stop losses of the retail trader (who probably uses a discount platform) is beyond ridiculous.

Does it matter to you where an ant has decided to store its food? Do you wake up every morning telling yourself, "Today is the day I raid that squirrel's food stash"? Of course not! That is what precisely you are assuming though when you say your stop losses are being hunted by other traders and this is why you use "mental" ones. Yes, using mental stop losses is "mental" for a beginner trader. In more than one sense.

This myth has been perpetuated thanks to poor mindset on the part of unsuccessful traders. Rather than accept responsibility that they are determining poor stop loss levels, surely, it must be someone else's fault that they lose money! These traders cannot be blamed for this, it is out of their control! Take a moment to think about the beliefs these traders possess and how it contradicts the true nature of making money via trading.

Correct SL Levels

Placing stop losses is a skill that you will get better at as time goes on. You will probably have the majority of your SLs tripped before price goes in the original direction quite a lot in the beginning. Determining SL levels is a combination of understanding S/R, the volatility of the instrument and a gut feeling which comes with experience and errors.

The true definition of an SL is "the point beyond which if the price were to move your entry doesn't make sense anymore." This is a rather vague statement that doesn't help us when we're starting out, no matter how correct it is. Start off by placing your SL order under or over the closest key S/R levels to your entry point. Why key S/R level?

Well if you recall what constitutes a key level, you will recall why this level would act as a barrier for price. Key S/R levels are the best options for your SL levels in a balanced environment. In a highly imbalanced environment, you can use a more dynamic level like the 20 EMA to inform your stop less level. In other words, place it beyond the 20 EMA. If you're using a crossover strategy, you can place it below the crossover point as well (in appropriate environments).

The volatility of the instrument determines how far below or above you place the stop loss order. More volatile instrument require greater breathing room than less volatile ones. When starting out, it is recommended you choose a slightly less volatile instrument. To get an idea of an instrument's volatility, observe how cleanly it respects key S/R levels when it retests them in different environments. Can you draw a relatively thin zone to mark the key level? Or is the zone wide? The wider it is, the more volatile the instrument. Take into account a large number of bars when determining this to avoid any recency bias (that is overvaluing the present).

Position Sizing

This is another area where beginners get tripped up. There's all sort of entry strategies out there involving pyramiding and scaling. It always pays to keep things as uncomplicated as possible. As such, leave the pyramiding, etc. to more experienced traders. Simply enter your full position size upfront.

How do you determine position size though? Well this is a relatively straightforward task and we'll use the example below:

Account size: 10,000 $

R: 0.25% or 25$

SL distance: 10 points

Position size= (R/SL)= 25/10= 2.5 units

The idea is the maximum loss you can sustain on this trade is the R amount. This is the simplest way to approach position sizing.

Take Profit Levels

Take profits can be approached in two different ways, unlike SLs where your only concern is determining the close key S/R level.

For beginners, a "set and forget" strategy is highly recommended. A set and forget strategy means you pick an SL, you pick your TP and then do nothing except observe the market as it moves towards either of those levels. You don't close out the trade at any time, and instead wait for one of those levels to be hit to exit the market.

TP Levels

Your TP level will simply be the place where, once price reaches it, you will make a pre-determined R multiple on the trade. When you have lots of data (at least 100 trades), you will know exactly which multiple makes you the most money and can calculate the level accordingly.

For the first 100, picking a 2R level is appropriate. Once you have enough data, you may realize that a 1.5R TP level increases your hit rate as well as your overall profit or maybe a 3R level decreases your hit rate but increases profits. Either way, you must understand, your first 100 trades are for the purposes of gathering data only. This is why it is crucial you keep your risk as low as possible.

These data gathering trades should not be on a live account as we'll see in the next chapter. For now though, let us look at how you calculate the TP price level. The calculation is the exact same formula as the SL one.

> Account size: 10,000$
>
> R: 0.25% or 25$
>
> TP: 2R or 50$

Position Size: 2.5 units

TP distance from entry point= (TP/Position Size)= (50/2.5)= 20 points.

So in the above scenario, if you entered a long position at $100 and have placed your SL at 10 points, your positions size is 2.5 units, your SL sell order is placed at $90 and your TP sell order is placed at $120.

An Alternative

The set and forget is what you ought to start with in the beginning. Once you've placed over 200 or so trades, you can begin experimenting with your TP levels. You see, to make the most money possible, it is essential to let your winners run. To let them run, you will need to evaluate the upcoming S/R and determine whether price is likely to break through it or not.

This obviously requires a degree of emotional detachment from the result of your trade. If you've already made 2R on the trade, will you be strong enough to hold on for a further potential 5R? How would you react if it went up to 5R and then swerved back below 2R? Only you can answer this honestly and this is why it is recommended to stick to the set and forget method for at least 200 trades.

This concludes our look at the basics of SL and TP levels. Remember, once you've gathered data over 100 trades, you will need to analyze them to see what hit rate and R multiple makes you the most money. You might need to extend your TP level and reduce your hit rate or reduce your TP level and extend your hit rate. Ultimately, all that matters is which scenario maximizes your profit (not how many trades you were correct on or some such).

We're finally ready to put together everything we've learned into a full-fledged swing trading plan. The next chapter will delve into this and by the end of it, you will be ready to trade!

CHAPTER 3:
TECHNICAL ANALYSIS AND FUNDAMENTAL ANALYSIS

Technical Analysis

In forex trading, technical analysis refers to the framework used by most trades to study the movement of prices, especially for short term traders. The theory behind technical analysis is that one can predict the current trading conditions and possible future price movements form analyzing the past price movements. Theoretically speaking, the main support of technical analysis is that the prices absorb all the information in the market. If therefore the prices reflect all the information that has affected the trade, then one can use price action to trade. History tends to repeat itself, and technical analysis follows the saying. Technical analysts study the charts and history in order to identify the patterns that are similar, and traders use the information with the belief that the currencies will act the same as the past.

Technical analysis involves studying the past price actions in an effort to identify similarities and drawing conclusions on the possible future movements. The nature of the forex market is that it operates 24 hours a day. Therefore, there is a lot of information and data that one can use to analyze the future price movements. The information used during technical analysis is statistical and the data being analyzed can be visualized and quantified using graphs and charts. The traders and analysts use indicators, technical studies, and other tools of analysis to gather the information. Summarily, technical analysis follows two things 1) identifying the trends, and 2) identifying resistance/ support through the analysis of timeframes on the price chart. The forex market can only move in three directions namely up, down or sideways. The prices typically follow a zigzag trend, and consequently, the price action can only have two states; the range and the trend. The range is when the price zigzag moves sideways while the trend is when the zigzag goes high (bull trend/ uptrend, or when it goes down (bear rend/ downtrend)

The importance of technical analysis

The main importance of technical analysis is that a trader can determine the where and when of entering or exiting the market and more so the latter. Some people say that one cannot get any value from analyzing the historical prices. Such traders follow the random walk theory whereby all markets are efficient, and they respond to changes in a random manner. Therefore, one cannot predict the future. Great investors including Warren Buffett heavily dispute the random walk theory and state that it is almost impossible for markets to be fully efficient. Inefficiencies are the opportunity makers that help the traders to capitalize on the movement of prices in the forex trade.

Analyzing price action using technical analysis tools helps one to make more informed decisions while trading.

The financial markets such as foreign exchange are not easy to analyze. These markets are influenced heavily by a wide selection of factors such as the monetary policies made by the central banks, governmental fiscal policies and other internal factors determined by the consumers and producers. Analyzing all the different factors and identifying how the influence the assets in the market can be a tough task. It is equally important that we note the ease at which a trader can make errors when analyzing a large number of factors. This particularly affects the inexperienced traders and those who have limited focus and time. The technical analysis helps the trader to focus on just one piece of crucial data which is the price movement. The analysis then offers traders; A way of judging the charts, identifying potential trade setups and managing them.

Technical analysis indicators

Technical indicators are used to mathematically analyze the connection between different elements on a chart in order to help traders predict the future prices. Many trading platforms have the indicators programmed on to their bodies. The most popular technical analysis indicators include:

Trend indicators: Average Directional Index (ADX), Moving Average (MA), Moving Average Convergence/Divergence (MACD), Ichimoku Kinko Hyo, and Parabolic SAR Indicator

Momentum: Relative Strength Index (RSI), Williams % range (%R), and Stochastic Oscillator

Volume: Money Flow Index, On-Balance Volume, and Accumulation/Distribution line

Volatility: Average True Range (ATR), Standard Deviation, and Bollinger Bands (BB)

How a trader can use technical analysis

One of the theories of technical analysis is that all markets are chaotic; therefore no one is sure of the changes that will occur next, but the patterns of price movement are not absolutely random. This is to say that on every chaotic situation there is an identifiable pattern that repeats itself in most cases (mathematical chaos theory).

The type of chaotic behavior observed in the forex market can be illustrated as that in the weather forecast. No one can say for sure that certain conditions will precede, but they can identify the probabilities and use them to draw almost true conclusions. A trader will admit that he/she has no guarantee in predicting the true price movements. As such, one should understand that successful trading is not all about being accurately right; it is about determining the probabilities and making trades when the odds are favorable. One part of determining the probabilities involves predicting the expected direction of the market. The next step involves predicting the entry and exit points. However, the trader should not forget the risk-reward ratio.

Although traders use the technical analysis indicators, there is no magical combination that can guarantee a trader full time wins. Some of the secrets identified by traders and analysts as keys to successful trading include good risk management programs, the ability to stay rational, and high-level discipline. Every trader can predict right and win, but it will not always be the case. If a trader does not have a good risk management strategy, he/she will not stay profitable in the long term even if they conduct a thorough technical analysis.

Fundamental Analysis

In the foreign exchange, fundamental analysis refers to the act of trading in the market based on the analysis of the global aspects that determine the demand and supply of currencies. A sizeable number of traders use both the fundamental and the technical analysis together to determent the when and where to trade. However, the traders tend to favor one over the other based on their individual investment plans and goals. To be precise, fundamental analysis studies aspects such as political forces, economic forces, and socials forces that may affect the asset. Many traders find ease in predicting the movement of prices while using supply and demand as an indicator. In simpler terms, the trader using fundamental analysis has to identify the economies that are blossoming and those that are stuck. As such, the trader has to know the whys and how an aspect will impact the trade, for instance, unemployment rates. The rates of unemployment affect the economy and the monetary policies implemented by the government and central banks, therefore, affecting the levels of demand and supply of the nation's currency worldwide.

Traders that use fundamental analysis pay attention to the overall state of a nation's economy and identify factors such as interest rates GDP, international trade, manufacturing, and international trade among others. The impact of these factors on the currency affects the price of the currency on the forex trade. The bottom line of fundamental analysis in the forex trade and also other markets is that an asset can have a price that differs from its actual value. Consequently, markets may misprice, underprice or overprice an asset in the short term. Fundamental analysts claim that despite misquote of the currency, an asset will still go back to its actual price indicating its true value. Then we can say that the bottom line of traders who use fundamental analysis to gauge assets are looking for trading opportunities through analyzing the value of the asset, the current price and the possibility of change.

The main difference between fundamental analysis and technical analysis is that fundamental analysis pays attention to all other factors of affecting the trade apart from the price while the technical analysis focuses on the price only. As such, the technical analysis is very handy for short term traders such as those in day trading while the fundamental analysis is beneficial for the long term traders such as those in the swing trading. The analysis of fundamental foreign exchange factors answers the long term questions.

Fundamental analysis tools

Fundamental analysis is done via different tool, and the most used ones include the financial news media, the economic calendar, and historical fundamental data. The financial news media gives news podcasts that update the traders of any major geopolitical and economic developments. That might affect the market directly or indirectly.

The economic calendar helps the trader to assess the date and time schedules of the release of data, either major or minor, that might affect the currencies.

Historical fundamental data is useful to the trader because it is enabling them to determine the trends in indicators. The traders can also analyze how a currency reacts to certain economic information release. This can be done by analyzing the behavior of the currency in the wake of previous similar releases and decisions.

There also other sources that one may use to base his/her opinion and they include the central banks, weather, and seasonality.

Central banks are probably one of the most charged sources of fundamental trading. This is because, they have a long list of actions they can take in finance, for instance, changing the interest rates (raising them or lowering them), maintaining the rates, making suggestions about the possible changes, the introduction of new policies, revaluation of the currency among others. The fundamental analysis of central banks usually involves thorough poring through speeches and statements made by central banks and attempt to predict their next moves.

One might wonder how the weather affects the forex exchange yet they seem unrelated in all ways. There are types of weather that can affect currencies in different countries. For example, in the winter season, a snow stomp in a country may drive the costs of natural gas up because it will be on high demand for heating homes. Also, there are certain weather situations that affect the value of good for example droughts, hurricanes, floods, and tornados. Some of these weather events are unpredictable to a large extent, but it would not hurt for one to check the weather channels and identify the weather unfolding.

Seasonality might be related to weather, but in this case, it is about some factors unrelated to weather. Seasonality means a period of time or rather time series. In trade, there are seasons that are good for selling while others are good for holding assets. For instance, in December, many investors sell off their securities if they have been declining throughout the year so that they can claim capital losses on tax. Sometimes, it is beneficial for a trader to exit a position before the selloff at the end of the year begins. Other seasons include the beginning of the year (January effect), and the end of the month (Month-end rebalancing.)

Fundamental analysis indicators

There are many indicators used in fundamental analysis, and they vary according to the nation. Currency traders use the indicators to assess the current and future state of the economy in the country. Some of the indicators include; Gross Domestic Product, trade balance, Currency account, employment data, inflation, and retail sales. Some of these indicators may help the trader to idealize what the future release will look like. Again, some of the indicators lead others in signaling the upturn or downturn of the economy. They include durable goods orders numbers, Producer Price Index, and purchasing manager surveys.

Some of the geopolitical events that can affect the forex market include elections, war, change of powers and natural disasters.

Fundamental analysis: Trading on the news

Some traders using the fundamental analysis follow data releases and economic news to initiate (enter) or liquidate (exit) the short term trades. They base their decision on the results of the release. It may sound easy to trade on fundamental news, but a trader should be aware that in most cases, the market does not react as expected. A number of times, the market will go to the opposite direction of what the traders anticipated.

When trading on the news, the traders use volatility strategies that involve the sale and purchase of options. The options are helpful in retaining a neutral position hence appreciating regardless of the direction that the market moves.

Traders also take advantage of the news related volatility when they trade with fundamentals by establishing a short and a long position in one pair and then close each side when the news is released.

Many professional traders avoid holding a large position just before a significant economic release. This is because the volatility associated with news release could initiate stop positions on any side.

Trade fundamental analysis allows a trader to have a deeper understanding of the ways in which the market reacts to events. Combining the technical analysis and the fundament information gives the trader an edge over the traders that are using one method.

Approaches to fundamental analysis

Keep in mind that Foreign exchange prices are influenced by the microeconomic and the macroeconomic data, geopolitical events, and the linkages. As seen earlier, the factors include GDP, Employment statistics, trade balances, and interest rates among others.

Top-Down Analysis

The top-down analysis starts with an analysis of the broad brush factors of macroeconomics and aggregates of data that works downwards. The traders narrow and refine the searches to only the pairs that present a potential for profit.

Bottom-Up analysis

Unlike the top-down analysis, the bottom-up analysis starts by analyzing the pair of currencies and then working upwards to the aggregate macroeconomics information.

Interest rates and balance of trade

These are some of the key drivers of currency and their prices. For example, if a country has surplus trade balance, then it means that the demand for services and goods is very high. Consequently, there will be a greater demand for the nations' currency thus increasing the relative value. Also, higher relative interest rates result in cash inflows, therefore, driving the value of the currency up.

Forces driving the demand and supply

These forces have a significant impact on how the commodities are valued. For instance, an occurrence of international war may lead to an increased demand for the metals used to manufacture ammunition and armaments, therefore, driving the prices up.

CHAPTER 4:
MOVING AVERAGES

Moving averages are another very popular and relatively simple trading tool that can be used by a swing trader. They can assist you in getting a good entry on a stock and further help you to stay in a position to take advantage of a long-term trend. They can also provide a good signal for when you should make an exit.

Moving averages come in 2 primary types: simple and exponential. Both of these moving averages can be calculated using different periods of time. The longer the time period used, the more likely the average will lag behind a stock price in an uptrend or downtrend. Let's start by looking at the difference between the simple and exponential moving averages, and then look at different time periods, and then, finally, consider how best to use them with your swing trading strategies.

Simple vs. Exponential Moving Averages

The difference between the simple moving average (SMA) and the exponential moving average (EMA) can be significant and your choice of which one you choose to use can make an impact on your trading. An SMA is calculated by starting with a period of time. Let's use 20 days as an example. You take the closing price for each of the previous 20 days, add these price numbers together, and then divide by 20. This gives you the average price for those 20 days. The next day you repeat the same process with the new set of numbers: the oldest day from your previous calculation gets dropped out because it is no longer in your 20-day range and the most recent closing price replaces it. As each day passes, you calculate a new 20-day SMA number that you can plot on a graph against the time. For the 50-day and the 200-day SMAs, you go through the same process with the corresponding number of days.

If the stock price you are plotting is constantly moving down, then the moving average prices get dragged lower as well. This gives you a trendline that you can monitor for trend changes. In our example, if the price reverses and starts to move higher, then the stock price will eventually cross the moving average, which has been lagging behind the current price movement. This cross provides a possible indicator of a change in sentiment.

Figure 8.5 shows a plot of Micron Technology, Inc. (MU) trending lower with the moving averages following the price down until it starts to reverse. On August 14th, MU's price crosses over the 20-day SMA. This is a sign of a possible change in investor sentiment with a new uptrend beginning. In our MU example, the price consolidates (churns sideways) for almost 2 weeks until the price starts to break above the 50-day SMA. After this event, the price trend change is clearly established and MU's stock price moves higher.

The chart of MU also shows how for a number of times the 20-day SMA acts as a support as the stock moves higher with waves of buying and selling. This illustrates how moving averages can be used to get a good entry in a trade and also to keep you in the trade in order to maximize profits.

The exponential moving average calculation is a little more complicated so I will not provide an explanation of it in this book. The formulas used are readily available on the Internet. The important thing to know when comparing the 2 different moving averages is that the EMA is more sensitive to recent changes in the price of the stock. This means that the EMA will react more quickly and, depending upon the situation, may or may not be good.

Because the EMA reacts faster when the price changes direction, it can provide an earlier signal of a possible change in trend. But, especially during times of higher volatility, this quicker reaction can also give the wrong signal. Stocks move in waves regardless of what direction they are moving: up, down or sideways. If a stock in a downtrend starts to bounce higher after a wave of selling, the EMA could start pointing up and potentially send a signal that there is an overall change in direction of the stock's price. This may not be the case if it is just a temporary bounce higher before continuing on a downtrend. Therefore this early indicator can result in a false trend change signal.

Because the SMA moves more slowly, it can keep you in a winning trade longer by smoothing out the inevitable bounces or pullbacks that normally occur during a long-term trend. Conversely, this slower moving trend line may also keep you in a trade when the trend has actually changed, so you may have to use other tools or fundamental analysis to decide if this trend is changing to the other direction. You will more often use the SMA when you are in your trades for longer durations and you are thus wanting to stay with a trend for as long as possible.

Due to the different levels of sensitivity between the 2 types of moving averages, you should consider adjusting which one to use based on the particular market environment. In volatile markets, where prices are bouncing up and down, an SMA may be a better tool. In less volatile market conditions, you would consider using the EMA to get earlier entry signals on trend changes.

Referring to Figure 8.6, you can see the difference between using the 20-day SMA versus the 20-day EMA. You'll notice that the EMA gives a slightly earlier signal as the MU price first crosses the faster reacting moving average. In this case, you may have got a slightly lower entry price on the trade, however, given the great run on MU it would not have made a big difference in your total return on the trade.

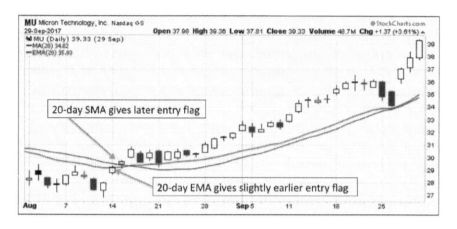

Moving Average Time Periods

As a swing trader using moving averages tools, you will need to consider what periods of time you want to use that give the best signals for your trading style. The first thing you should do is to stay with some of the periods that are commonly used by traders and computers. As I have discussed already, these moving averages work as technical indicators because they are, in effect, self-fulfilling prophecies. Many other traders and machines are looking at the same indicators and they work in part because of that fact.

The shorter the number of days used to calculate the moving average, the sooner you will see a change in direction because the short time periods more strongly reflect current price action.

Like the EMA, these shorter time frames can be good in identifying a shift in sentiment between the buyers and sellers, but they can also give false signals by reflecting the waves of buying and selling that occur within the typical wave action movements of a stock's price.

The most common periods used by swing traders are 20-day, 50-day and 200-day SMAs. Because traders are watching price movements in relation to these averages, they usually offer areas of support and resistance. The 200-day SMA is highly revered and normally provides the strongest level of support when a stock is selling off and the strongest level of resistance when a stock is starting to move higher from a low.

Traders also use the percentage of stocks in the market that are trading above their 200-day average as a gauge to determine the overall health of the stock market. The higher the percentage of stocks above their 200-day SMA, the more the overall market is biased to trending higher, therefore, the better trades for a swing trader may be long trades versus going short.

Below are some further thoughts to consider in developing your strategies related to using moving averages when swing trading:

The 20-day SMA is a good tool to use for a short-term swing trade. In a trending stock, the price action will often respect this level and it will also quickly identify a shift in sentiment and thus a reversal in trend.

The 20-day EMA is a faster reacting tool that can be used for short-term swing trades. It can get you into a trade earlier but in more volatile markets, it can also give you a false trend reversal signal.

The 50-day SMA is also a popular gauge for a longer-term swing trade and it will allow you to ride a potentially profitable trade longer in order to make additional gains. It is a good intermediate balance between the shorter 20-day and the longer 200-day SMAs.

The 200-day SMA represents almost 1 year of past price action (there are about 250 trading days in a year). In a down trending stock, this SMA may provide significant support and therefore be a good entry for a long position due to it being a very popular level for traders (remember the discussion on self-fulfilling prophecies). The risk on this sort of trade is when the price finds a support level just below the 200-day SMA and the trader is then stopped out.

The Golden Cross and the Death Cross

One other way to use moving averages to determine a directional price change is to watch for what traders refer to as a "golden cross" or a "death cross". This indicator uses the 50-day and 200-day SMAs. For example, let's consider a stock that has been in a long-term downtrend. Due to this trend, the 50-day moving average is creating a line that is below the 200-day SMA line. A golden cross signal on this stock will occur when the 50-day SMA crosses the 200-day moving average from below to above. When this happens, it is an indication that the negative sentiment is possibly changing with the downtrend in price shifting to an uptrend. This cross happens because the 50-day SMA is reflecting more current price action while the 200-day SMA is lagging further behind, reflecting prices that are further in the past.

The death cross is the opposite of the golden cross. It occurs when a stock is in a general uptrend and the price action starts to trend lower. Once again, the faster-reacting 50-day SMA starts to turn down faster than the slower reacting 200-day SMA and they eventually cross. The 50-day SMA crosses from above the 200-day SMA to below it, showing a change in sentiment and stock price direction.

Moving Averages in Range-Bound Stocks and Markets

As a swing trader, you need to be aware that SMA and EMA tools do not work well in markets or in stocks that are trading in a limited range (where the price makes relatively small moves between support and resistance). This type of market or stock is referred to as being "range-bound", and the price action is commonly referred to as "churning". In these range-bound trading cases, all of the different time period SMA and EMA lines ripple sideways between levels of support and resistance. The price action does not respect these lines, therefore, these tools are most effective when trends are occurring: either higher or lower.

How to Use Moving Averages

You can also monitor these averages once you have entered a trade in order to help you to decide whether to exit a trade completely at a target price or to take some of the position off at one target and continue to hold the rest as the stock price continues to move in your favor. This is referred to as "scaling out" and will be discussed later in the book.

The SMA can be used to find a potential area of support or resistance. For example, if you are holding a short position, you might consider covering all or some of that short position as the price of the stock approaches the 200-day SMA, which is watched by many traders and trading machines as an area of significant support.

Moving averages can be used as an indicator to enter a trade, to exit a trade and to stay in an existing trade. Therefore, it is a good tool in your arsenal when markets and/or stocks are trending up or down.

CHAPTER 5:

BOLLINGER BANDS

Finding points where true reversals can occur is important, but so is locating levels of support and resistance. Bollinger bands can be added to your stock charts and help you determine what these price ranges are. Note that Bollinger bands are dynamic, so each day the level of support and resistance is going to be adjusted. But this will give you a more accurate picture of what's going on rather than just relying on drawing straight lines through the charts.

We've also denoted some interesting candles.

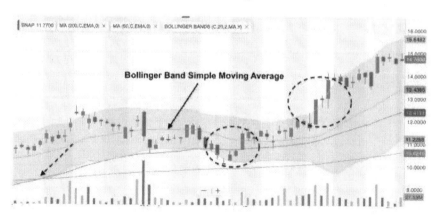

When you see stock prices on the edge of the Bollinger bands that indicates that the prices are over bought or oversold, because they are one or two standard deviations from the mean. However that doesn't mean a trend reversal is coming. On the left side of the chart, notice that two of the candles actually fall outside the

Bollinger bands – and so they are more than two standard deviations away from the 20 day mean. And indeed, after that there was a short term decline in prices. However that seems to be more of a retracement. The golden cross held true and the stock has continued to climb.

If you look at the first dotted oval, you will see that the bottom candle also falls outside the range of the Bollinger bands. That would be an excellent buying point for the stock. It was followed by a strong upturn.

Don't blindly make trading moves when you see prices fall outside the Bollinger band. Use multiple indicators to look for the trend and trade with the trend.

One thing to look for is the width of the Bollinger bands. If they get wide, that is telling you that the stock is gaining more volatility. When they are tightening, that means there is less volatility, but that can be followed by large breakouts to one side or the other.

Looking at Netflix, we can see that this kind of phenomenon might be setting up:

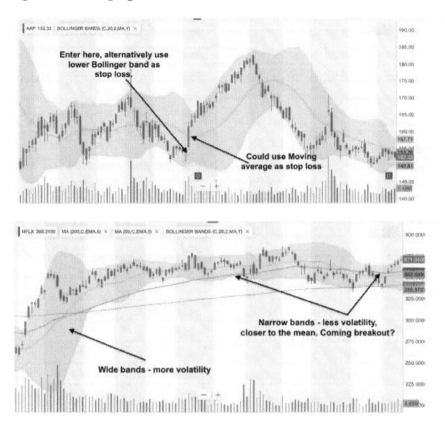

Look for narrow bands because a breakout move is possible in the future. Volatility can expand after a period of narrow bands.

One of the ways that you can use Bollinger bands is to look for opportunities to enter trades. If you are looking for the stock price to increase, you can wait for it to hit the lower Bollinger band, or even to fall slightly below it. If you can confirm with signals of a coming uptrend, this can be a good opportunity to buy, with a trigger to sell at the level of the upper Bollinger band.

Sometimes the stock will be trading above or below the mean, but you'll see it reverting to the mean as it goes up and down. Although these represent smaller opportunities to profit, when it reverts to the mean this could be a buying opportunity, and then you look for it to rise again to hit the upper Bollinger band, and sell at that point.

Alternatively you could short the stock at the top and wait for it to revert to the mean on the way back down.

When the security is in a big trend, you can use the 20 period moving average to set your stop-loss. In this example, Apple is making a big move up in price, and you can see all the candles are well above the mean.

Following the strong uptrend, we see an equally strong downtrend. Notice how closely the candles in both cases are following the outer Bollinger bands.

True Range and Average True Range

True range is calculated at each trading day (or point you are using) and is taken to the largest of one of the three following quantities:

- Difference between the current days high price and its low price

- The difference between the previous days closing price and the current days high price

- The difference between yesterdays closing price and todays low price

This is a measure of volatility in the share price. It can then be averaged using a 14 day moving average to give the average true range. Average true range increases with increasing volatility and decreases with when volatility decreases. Average true range is used to determine exit points. However, note that while the true range gives a measure of volatility, it does not indicate price direction.

The Chandelier exit uses true range to calculate an exit point by calculating a multiple of the true range, then subtracting that from the highest high that occurred after entering the trade. So it would define a stop loss point, typically using 3 x the average true range subtracted from the high.

ADX and Moving Average Convergence/Divergence (MACD)

Directional movement indices are a way to measure the momentum that bulls or bears have in the market. However these usually aren't used alone, instead the difference between the two, which is called the ADX is used to measure the strength of a trend. In the chart below, we see the ADX is plotted below the Apple year to date stock chart. The ADX shows the strength of the trend with positive being an upward trend since it's the difference between the directional movement indexes for bulls pushing prices above the previous days high minus the directional movement index for bears.

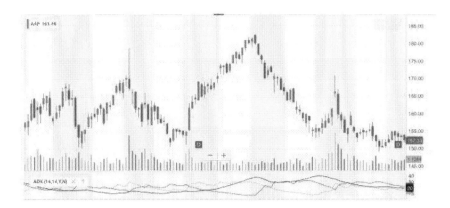

The way that a trader will use the ADX, is to confirm that a real trend exists. Of course in this example we have picked an obvious trend to highlight, but not all trends are that obvious, but you can confirm by looking for movement in the ADX. Entry and exit points can be selected by looking for cross overs in the directional movement indices. When the bullish index crosses over the bearish line that is a buy signal if you are long on the stock.

MACD is a trend following indicator based on exponential moving averages. It takes the 12 period moving average and then subtracts the 26 period moving average. The MACD includes a signal line and when it crosses above the signal line, this is taken as a buy signal if you are hoping for a rise in stock price. When it crosses below the signal line that is a sell signal (reverse if shorting the stock). In the chart below we have used the MACD with the chart for Apple stock.

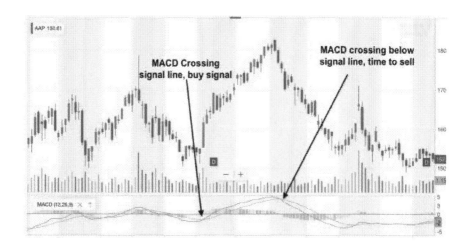

Choose your indicators

As we mentioned above, drowning yourself in multiple indicators is probably not going to be very productive. The best approach to use is to pick 2 or 3 and stick with them. The MACD is one of the most effective indicators, but simply looking for cross overs between short and long period moving averages works quite well. You can combine this with looking at candles to make effective buy and sell decisions. But remember this is not a precise science and the fact that people's behavior and the stock market in general are chaotic, and also impacted by news often quite dramatically, means not all of your trades are going to work despite using every tool that is available. The only thing you can really accomplish is tipping the odds in your favor, so that you end up with more wins than losses. The point here is you shouldn't get too down when trades go bad.

CHAPTER 6:
TRUNCATED PRICE SWING STRATEGY

This swing and day trading strategy can be used on its own, though should really be used in conjunction with other strategies. This strategy gets you looking at trends and reversals, and also introduces an entry technique—the "consolidation breakout"—that's incorporated into many of the strategies that follow as well.

The strategy gets you into a move early, risk is relatively small and it aligns your trades with the trend (or with the potentially emerging trend). It's used to take advantage of the swings which occur every single day, so the strategy provides ample trade signals.

While no system is perfect, this trading strategy often provides high rewards for the risk and shows you quite quickly if you're on the right side of the market or not—saving you time so you can get out and move on to the next trade if it doesn't work out. Some potential flaws of this trading method are discussed at the end of the chapter.

A truncated move, the basis of this strategy, is a price move that doesn't reach the previous price move extreme. There are truncated moves that indicate a trend is continuing, and those that indicate a reversal. In a downtrend, if a rally fails to reach the previous high, it's a truncated price move. In an uptrend if a pullback fails to reach the prior swing low, it's a truncated price move. In both these cases, the truncated price move indicates the overall trend is continuing.

If the overall trend is up and a wave higher fails to reach the last swing high, it's a truncated price move and indicates a possible reversal, or a consolidation in price. If the trend is down and a wave lower fails to reach the low of the last swing low, it's a truncated price move and indicates a possible reversal higher, or a price consolidation. The truncated price moves in these last two cases violate the basic tenants of trends—higher highs and higher lows for uptrends, and lower highs and lower lows for downtrends—indicating the trend is in jeopardy.

I especially like this strategy near the open—the European open, or during the European/US overlap period—but it can be used during any of the recommended day trading times. Assume the EURUSD opens at 1.3000 and drops 20 pips near the start of the European session, moves higher and then starts heading back to test the low at 1.2980. But this current price swing fails to reach that low before heading higher again. Simply put, we have a higher low—a truncated move—and a potential trade.

It provides a low risk opportunity to get long.

The chart below shows the EURUSD on a 1-minute chart. This example

took place not long after the London open.

Focusing on the yellow area, which highlights the London session, the

EURUSD moves lower, higher, makes a new low and then rallies back toward the former high.. but it doesn't make it there. That's what we're watching for.

The price stalls below the former high, and I've marked that area with a

white rectangle. We know a short trade could be forthcoming, because if the price can't push through the former high, it's likely to head lower, even if temporarily.

A potential trade needs a "trigger." The trigger indicates exactly when a trade should be taken. This is where drawing a little rectangle around the price action helps.

In this example a small range (rectangle) is created below the old high. A break below the rectangle (very short-term support) signals the truncation is in place and a short trade can be taken. While not all trades are this successful, the market moved aggressively lower after that small range was broken.

To summarize, for an entry we're watching for any move that's heading to

test a high or low, but doesn't make it there. Once the price stalls and starts to reverse away from the high or low, we're watching for a trigger which initiates our trade— this could be a candlestick pattern (such as an engulfing pattern, discussed earlier in the book), or a collection of bars and then a breakout from those bars (consolidation breakout).

My preferred method entry is the consolidation breakout—I use it for many different strategies. In order to get a trade trigger, the price needs to pause just below a prior high or just above a prior low so some very short-term support and resistance can form. Draw a rectangle similar to the one on the chart and await a breakout from it.

Stops are placed just above (1 pip plus the spread for day trading, 5 pips plus spread for swing trading) the truncated high or just below (1 pip for day trading, 5 pips for swing trading) the truncated low which keeps the risk in pips usually fairly small (relative to the surrounding price action).

In the example above, we enter short at 1.3020 and our stop is 1.3026. Add a couple pips, so the stop in this case is closer to

1.3028. The profit target for this strategy can be based on multiple factors. One option is to set the profit target at a location which presents a 2:1 reward to risk ratio. In the case above, our stop is 8 pips, so our target would be 16 pips from our entry price. If the price movement is a little sluggish, use a 1.75:1 target. If your stop is 8 pips, your target is 14 pips with this reward: risk ratio.

Using a larger reward: risk ratio may result in a bigger profit, but the trades last longer and the target is less likely to be hit. Since signals for this strategy occur frequently throughout the day, getting in and out swiftly with a 2:1 (or 1.75:1) reward to risk is beneficial since you can quickly begin looking for another trade.

Making two or three trades with a 2:1 reward to risk is better than making one trade with a 3:1 ratio. Take a quick profit and move on. I've used many other methods for exiting this trade, but often find that no matter what profit target method is used, the ratio normally ends up near 1:75 to 2:1, therefore, to keep things simple just use the 2:1 (reward :risk) ratio under most market conditions. In times when volatility is decreasing, use a slightly smaller target.

The 2:1 reward to risk assumes the entry is actually attained near the actual price trigger (consolidation breakout or engulfing pattern). Regardless of where the actual entry takes place (the price you get the position at) the stop should always be placed above the truncated high or below the truncated low and the profit target is then placed at a distance which is equal to two times the risk from the trigger/breakout point. Hopefully this is the same as your trade price, but if you happen to miss the entry point by five pips to due slippage or slow reflexes, the originally calculated stop and profit target shouldn't be adjusted for these 5 pips.

If you get a lot of slippage on your order, don't adjust the stop and profit target to reflect it, keep the original stop and profit target. Just because you missed your entry point by five pips doesn't mean the strategy should be altered to suit your predicament. If you miss a trade, let it go. There will be others. We don't want to start chasing the price, as this increases our risk (based on where the stop should be placed) and decreases the profit potential.

On the same day as the example above, three more signals pop-up (see chart below). For these, the trade triggers were engulfing patterns. Engulfing patterns, in addition to the "consolidation breakouts" method discussed prior, are a reliable trade trigger when using the truncated price swing strategy.

A bullish engulfing pattern is when an up-bar completely envelops the prior down-bar after a downward move. A bearish engulfing pattern is when a down-bar completely envelops the prior up-bar after an up move. The set-ups and patterns are marked on the chart below—the engulfing patterns are our entry signals and are marked by arrows on the chart.

Trade 2 is a lower high, and the trade signal is a bearish engulfing pattern.

Enter short as the pair moves below the low of the former bar. This gives a short entry price of 1.3012. The recent high 211 is at 1.3016 and our stop goes just above it, making it 1.3018 (6 pips of risk). The target is therefore, 12 pips below our entry price or at 1.3000. The market reaches 1.2997 so the trade is profitable.

Trade 3 appears right after exiting Trade 2. An aggressive bullish engulfing pattern triggers a long trade, on a higher low (truncated price swing). Enter long at 1.3006, which is one pip above the former bar. Stop is below the recent low (low of the bullish engulfing bar in this case) at 1.2997. Subtract one pip to make it 1.2996. The stop is therefore 10 pips and our target is 20 pips. Add the target to the entry price of 1.3006, giving a price target of 1.3026. The market reaches 1.30267 so the trade is profitable.

Trades 4 and 5 happen quickly. For trade 4 we get a bullish engulfing pattern, but the market then moves lower losing us 6 pips. We're still watching for a higher low, as we remain well above the prior low (trade 3 in this case) at this time. Another bullish engulfing pattern occurs and we enter long for trade 5. We go long at 1.3010, stop is 1.3005 and our target is therefore at 1.3020. The market moves up to 1.30236 so this trade is profitable.

This strategy worked well on this day using a one-minute chart. You don't need to use a one-minute chart though; use a 5 minute or even a daily chart. The trade setups are still the same, as shown on the daily chart below.

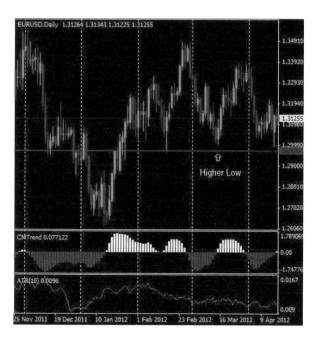

Regardless of the time frame, the rules are the same. You're looking for a higher low or a lower high and you want either a collection of bars which provide you with a trade trigger (consolidation breakout) or an engulfing pattern.

In the case of the daily EURUSD chart above, the trigger is an engulfing

pattern. The bullish engulfing pattern appeared right above the prior low, indicating a truncated move. Our entry point is 1.3090 as the "bullish" day surpasses the high of the former down day. Our stop is placed just below the recent low (5 pips below, since it's a swing trade) at 1.3000 (90 pips risk). The target is therefore 180 pips added to our entry price, to get 1.3270. This target is reached several days later.

The chart below is a daily AUDUSD chart. I've highlighted the trend with a white line to show the simple structure of truncated price moves—in this case there's a low, a move higher, a move down which creates a higher low and then a move back higher. Once you see the higher low, you want to trade the next move higher.

If you can get a good entry into this wave higher you stand a very good

chance of capturing a profit. In this example, many novice traders will wait till the price moves above the major high at approximately 1.04 to enter, but this entry gets you into the move too late.

As long as the price remains above the former lower (a potential higher low) look for a trigger which signals a move back higher; the primary triggers are a consolidation breakout or an engulfing pattern.

The chart below shows the zoomed-in version of the turning point on the

AUD/USD daily chart above. I've drawn a blue box around the consolidating price 214

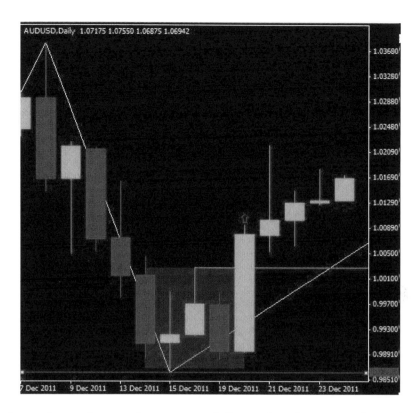

action where the market stopped dropping for several sessions. Since the price is still above the former low we're looking for entry signals to go long (buy).

In order to catch an up move we want to see some sort of bottoming process first. When the market moves sideways for at least three bars and then begins to move higher, that's the type of pattern we're looking for.

Our entry candle is marked by the small arrow and our entry price is marked by the horizontal line. On December 20 there's a big bar which moves higher than the highest point in the consolidation—the entry occurred at 1.0027. Remember signals are traded in real-time; don't wait for bars to close. On December

20th, as soon as the price rose above the highest price in the consolidation, a long trade is initiated.

Our stop loss goes below the recent 0.9862 low, marked by the horizontal line, making the stop 0.9857 (5 pips below the low). The risk is (1.0027-0.9857) 170 pips; our target is 2 x 170 pips = 340 pips, added to the breakout price, giving 1.0367. This target was hit a couple weeks later.

Truncation Strategy Considerations

The main down side of this strategy is that you don't know for sure if the pair is actually going to reverse. An uptrend is defined as "higher highs and higher lows" or in the case of a downtrend "lower lows and lower highs." This strategy jumps the gun in that it only requires a higher low to be present into order to jump into a long position, or only requires a lower high to enter a short position. That said, the trade set-up presents evidence the trend may be reversing (or continuing as the case may be) and the risk/reward indicates we can be wrong more often than we are right and still make a profit.

I advise focusing on short trades where the last swing low was lower than the former swing low, and the price is making a lower high. I advise focusing on long trades where the last swing high was higher than the former swing high and the price is making a higher low. In other words, **trade in the overall trending direction.** For example, in an uptrend when the price pulls back but stays above the former low. That's a signal I feel good about trading, and the target is likely to get hit. If the trend is up and then I get a lower-high and a trigger, that's a reversal signal (not a trend following signal). I may still trade it, but I'll often use a lower reward: risk such as 1.5:1 instead of the usual 2:1, because I want to get out quicker in case the uptrend re-establishes itself.

Day trade the strategy only during the recommended day trading times for the specific pair you're trading. This pattern is very common. You'll see it a lot, which potentially means lots of trades. You may opt to filter some trades out. Applying a filter with this strategy can be useful. For instance, choose to only take long trades when there's a dominant up trend, or to only take short trades when an overall downtrend is present. This is where understanding the other chapters will help you, especially being able to gauge shifting markets.

DON'T TRADE EVERY SIGNAL THAT COMES ALONG. Be selective and look at overall momentum. Be aware of the pair's daily statistics when day trading. If you get a trigger to go long when the EUR/USD is already up 130 pips 216 on the day (and it usually moves 100) then the odds of your target being hit even further outside the daily range isn't very likely.

Trade triggers and profit targets can also be customized based on the pairs you trade and patterns you notice. For example, you may find a 2:1 reward: risk is just out of reach, so a 1.75:1 or 1.5:1 is more favorable. Alternatively, a pair may be trending strongly, and 3:1 ratio are easily attainable for a time. Monitor conditions and adjust the strategy accordingly, typically though 2:1 reward to risk works quite well.

In hindsight it's easy to see the market made a higher low and that a long position should've been taken, or a lower high was made so a short position should've been taken. In real-time it'll be unknown whether the market is going to reverse or just pause before continuing on its current course. For this reason, the trade triggers are extremely important.

From my experience the best trade trigger is when the market pauses for several bars, moving predominately sideways, creating a consolidation as shown in the examples above. We then wait for a consolidation breakout and pounce.

Though, often there's no pause. The price simply snaps back the other way leaving you without a trade. The engulfing pattern allows you to capture some of those trades that the "consolidation breakout" trigger doesn't.

Both these patterns (consolidation breakout and engulfing pattern) need to be watched for **in real-time**. If the trend in the AUD/USD is up, you'll want to watch for pullbacks in price in order to buy into that uptrend. As long as the rate is above the prior low you have a potentially higher low. If the trigger develops, then you'll enter into a long trade. Seeing the trigger developed several bars ago may provide some analytical insight, but it's too late to be used for trading purposes.

Learning when to watch for triggers, being able to see the trigger develop and then pouncing on those opportunities will eventually become second-nature to you. At first though, it may be hard to spot the patterns in real-time; with patience and practice it'll happen.

CHAPTER 7:

MONEY MANAGEMENT

By now, you have learnt so much about trading. On top of learning about the basics of it such as: what trading is, how it works, who is a broker and the like, you have also learnt about the various successful swing trading strategies that you can apply. However, you are not there yet. You need to learn about one of the main challenges that plague the business of trading, and that is risk.

It doesn't matter how much knowledge you have about the markets, or how good you are at applying a successful strategy. If there is one thing that you cannot eliminate from the business of trading, that would be risk.

It is for that reason that I have found it extremely important to include this chapter as part of this book. This chapter is going to cover risk management, especially as it applies to trading.

Truth be told, risk management is a very wide subject. I could end up writing an entire book in the subject, but let's just save that for another time. And my guess is, you have little interest in learning all there is to risk management anyway. That is best left to bankers and other finance professionals. You are more likely to be interested in learning risk management tips that you can apply right away and become a better trader. And that is what this chapter will cover.

Let's begin our discussion by looking at one important concept – leverage.

The Concept Of Leverage In Trading

Earlier in this book, we talked about leverage, although briefly. We described it as a way of borrowing money from your broker so that you can control larger financial transactions than the amount you have available for trading. So let's dive deeper.

Leverage can be defined as a special type of loan that is extended to you as an investor, so that you can increase the returns form a certain type of investment. In other words, leverage is simply borrowing to invest more.

As an example, let us look at how leverage works in the world of real estate. Particularly, let us look at how mortgage financing works. When you want to buy a home valued at say $100,000, it is common practice to invest part of your money first and then borrow the rest.

So you may put up say $30,000 first and then borrow the remaining $70,000 from your bank to finance the rest of the purchase.

Now let us say that you bought the house purely for investment purposes. So, maybe in a year's time, the house grows in value to say $150,000. If you sell it and pay back the bank's money plus interest (let's say interest was 8% per annum), you will have made a profit of around $44,400. This is a whopping 148% return on investment.

That is the power of using leverage in your investments.

In trading, it works the same way. You open an account with your broker and deposit an amount in it. This amount which you invest upfront is always known as your margin. Then your broker will provide leverage so that you can magnify your investment.

The margin required will be calculated by the leverage that your broker is willing to provide. If your broker provides leverage of 500:1, this means that you can multiply the amount invested by five hundred. To calculate the margin required, use this formula

$$\text{Margin} = \frac{1 \quad X \quad 100\%}{\text{Leverage}}$$

So margin required for the above leverage is

$$= \frac{1 \quad X \quad 100\%}{500} \quad = \quad 0.20\%$$

This means that you will be required to have 0.20% of the total transaction value as margin. So if you wanted to transact a trade worth $100,000, then you would need to deposit $20 as the minimum amount to invest.

$$\frac{0.20\% \times 100,000}{100\%} \quad = \$20$$

If your account balance falls below the minimum amount that is required for your margin, perhaps if a trade went wrong and you lost a lot of money, then you will get what is called margin call.

So if you had deposited $100 in your account and you took a huge hit such that the money in your account fell below $20, then you will receive a margin call. A margin call is simply a message from your broker informing you that you all your positions have been closed out and that you need to deposit more money as margin so that you can resume trading.

Why are we having this long discussion about leverage?

High effective leverage happens to be one of the most common risk factors when it comes to trading. Leverage has the capacity to make you make a lot of money very fast, but at the same time, you could lose money just as fast, especially if you were wrong.

By effective leverage, I mean the amount of leverage that you are currently using. Your broker may be offering you the highest leverage possible (I've seen leverage as high as 2000:1), but you may decide to only use part of it as it suits you. For example, you may decide to use 100:1 because that's what your account can handle.

To calculate effective leverage, simply use the formula below

$$\text{Effective leverage} = \frac{\text{Total value of transaction}}{\text{Total trading capital}}$$

So, if you were transacting a trade worth $100,000, with $1,000 in your account, then your effective leverage would be 100:1 (or 100 times your deposit)

$$= \frac{\$ 100,000}{\$ 1,000}$$

If we applied this example in the Forex market (which is the main market where leverage is always this high), when trading one standard lot (which is worth $100,000) you are making $10 per pip. A pip is short form for price interest point. A pip is the value of each price movement in the Forex market. If the USD/JPY moved from 112.60 to 112.70, that would be considered a ten pip movement ($112.70 - 112.60$).

So a movement like this would be worth $100(10pips x $10 = $100).

A mini lot (which is worth $10,000) will earn you $1 per pip. So a price movement like the one above would be worth $10.

What the examples above prove is that effective leverage is what presents the most risk in trading. You should use effective leverage that is in line with the size of your account.

As a rule, the size of your account should be at least 100 times the amount you are risking per trade. From the examples above, trading one standard lot is better done with an account holding at least $10,000 as margin. Trading one mini lot is better done with an account holding at least $1,000 as margin.

Having looked at leverage in great depth, let us now look at some great tips for managing risk as a trader.

Tips For Managing Risk As A Trader

1. Make sure you have stop-loss orders in place

Previously, we talked about stop-loss orders when discussing swing trading strategies. So let's revisit the concept.

A stop-loss order is a special type of order that you place with your broker at the time of placing your trade, ordering him or her to automatically close off your trade at a small loss, should the market fail to move in the direction that you predicted.

It is the most basic type of risk management tool you can ever find in the financial markets.

Generally, you should get into the habit of placing a stop-loss order every time you place a trade in the market. This helps you protect your capital against unforeseen events that could result in a catastrophic financial loss to your account.

As a trader or investor, you should always assume that every trade that you place in the market carries risk of capital loss. Therefore, you owe it to yourself to keep that loss at a manageable level so that you can afford to trade in the future.

That is where a stop loss order comes in. Given the tools that we have just discussed, you are capable of calculating the risk of loss that comes with each trade and the amount you are willing to risk in each trade. Then, accompany every trade that you place with a stop loss order to ensure that you have managed the situation.

This is so important I will say it again; please avoid market orders. These are open orders that you can place in the market at whatever price there is and can sell at any time or price you want. This type of order leaves you exposed. It offers no protection against loss and the point of taking profit isn't defined as well.

In short, this type of order leaves you with no control of the situation. Instances where the markets move several points in a few seconds certainly do exist. If you trade with this type of order during such times, then you will be in a lot of trouble. Better place an order that takes care of the situation when it needs to.

You will save yourself a lot of financial heartache if you do. Don't say I didn't warn you.

2. Watch out for high volatility in the markets

Take a look at the charts below. They were both pulled out of the markets but at different times.

Which of these two markets do you suppose is more difficult to trade than the other?

If you guessed the first one, then you are very right.

The fact of the matter is that the markets will not behave the same at all times. Sometimes the market will be in a very good and predictable mood, which makes it easier for you and other investors to make money.

At times, the market can be very moody and unpredictable, in which case, making money becomes very difficult. Knowing the difference between these two times can give you a significant edge and increase your probability of making money in the end.

If you want to be able to trade profitably and with much ease, then you have to stay away from hostile market environments that a very difficult to understand and predict. You should stick to trading during periods when the market is trading uniformly, smoothly and predictably.

If you think about it, trading is like swimming in a river. Imagine for a moment that you are someone who loves to swim. You have a specific spot at the river where you and your friends love to swim, and have for years now. The spot is always calm and the water flows evenly and quietly.

Then one day, you arrive at that spot and you find that rain that fell upstream caused that place to flood and the river is flowing violently with huge rapids and some trees have even been carried away. Would you consider swimming at that spot? Of course, you wouldn't dream of doing that in your worst dreams. If you do so, chances of you drowning and losing your life are very high. And that is the same thing that happens in trading.

When you choose to trade during a time when prices are thrashing around violently and there is a lot of unpredictability in the market, then you are sure to drown. You will drown financially.

It is better to be patient until the market mood improves, and then you can be sure to start placing your bets. If you do so, you will be like a wise swimmer who only swims at the river when there are no floods or rapids, mainly because his or her life is at risk.

An angry market mood is risky for your wallet and will surely cannibalize your capital faster than you could imagine. Volatility or market mood can always be determined visually. You do not need special tools for this. If you see the prices moving uniformly, then you know it's time to play. If it's the opposite of that, then you should stay away.

3. Watch out for high spreads

Another risk factor in the financial markets is the spread.

In case you have forgotten, the spread is the difference between the asking price and the actual trading price of an asset or security.

It is how your broker makes his or her living – by taking a commission on every trade you place, whether you make money or not.

For the most part, a reputable broker will charge you fair

spreads. But still, you should keep a keen eye on it because there are instances where your broker may raise the spread. Sometimes it could be raised to some unbelievably high levels.

Take the example of the Forex market. The typical spread in this market from a reputable broker is roughly 1 to 2 pips (price interest points), as seen in the screenshot below:

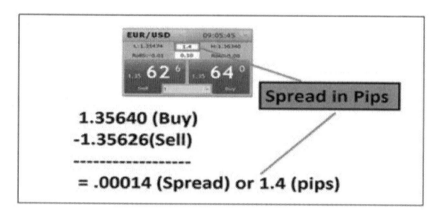

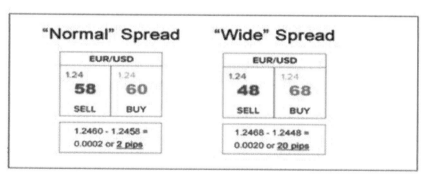

Your broker may do this for a number of reasons. For instance, your broker may raise the spread during times when liquidity is low. When there are few buyers and sellers in a market (which translates to low liquidity), your broker is obligated by law to step in and provide a market. This presents a huge risk for him and so, he may raise the spread to offset that risk.

Another reason he may do this is due to high volatility in the market. This is especially the case when it comes to periods of fundamental news releases. Due to the impact that news releases have on the markets and the fact news today is readily available, more and more people are becoming interested in trading news or fundamentals.

During periods of fundamental announcements, your broker may raise the spread, to account for the huge risk, which results from the huge volume of trading that occurs during such times.

What this means is that the risk is transferred to you as the trader or investor who decides to do business during such times.

Up to this point, what I've taught you is to carry out technical analysis as the way to inform your trading decisions. In my experience, I find no reason at all to increase your risk by trading during periods of high volatility such as when fundamental news is being released.

It is very vital that you keep the spreads as low as possible if you want an edge in this business. Huge spreads could end up eating into your profits thus crippling you in the long run.

4. Always maintain an acceptable risk-reward ratio

The risk-reward ratio is another part of every trade that should always be under your radar.

Risk reward-ratio can be defined as the measurement of the downside risk to the upside profit potential that a trade holds.

This is one of the key areas where many novice traders who fail to make money in the markets mainly go wrong. A study done by Daily fx researchers on traits of successful traders, highlighted wrong risk-reward ratios as the number one mistake made by most traders.

The study pointed out that on average; top traders were right 50 to 60 percent of the time. The study also showed that most traders were able to meet this number.

In short, most traders were just about as right as the top traders. So what made most of these traders lose? This was when an amazing discovery was made.

The top traders were able to make money because they kept a high risk reward ratio in all their trades. The losing traders allowed for exceptions and therefore most of their winning trades were outdone by the huge losses on their losing trades.

In short, a good risk reward ratio can mean the difference between losing and making money.

Take a look at the math of it. Let's assume that you maintained a risk reward ratio of 1:2 in all your trades. That means that for each risk you took, you were looking to make at least twice that amount in profit. If you happened to be right 50% of the time, would still make a nice profit.

Assume $500 risk per trade.

50% winners means 5 out of ten wins = $1000 x 5 = $5,000

50% losers means 5 out of ten losers =$500 x 5 = $2,500

Then subtract the losers from winners

$5,000 – $2,500 = $2,500

And you have **$2,500** in profit.

If you maintain a risk reward ratio of 1:1 using the example above, then you would break even. If you kept a risk reward ratio that is lower than that, then you would net losses every time.

This is also one of the reasons why setting a stop-loss order and a take-profit order ahead of time is very important. Doing this allows you to quantify the amount of risk that you are willing to take as well as the profit you anticipate. After doing this, you can literally walk away from your computer and not worry about anything else.

So, strive to ensure that every trade you are placing meets this requirement. Whenever you can, keep the risk reward ratio at least 1:2 in every trade you place.

You will be surprised at how it will improve your trading and make it so stress-free.

5. Position sizing

Along the same lines as watching out for the effective leverage that you are employing, you need to consider your position size very carefully.

Like I said, as a trader, you have to assume that every trade you place carries risk, no matter how promising it looks. If you fail to heed to this useful piece of trading wisdom, then you will be in for the biggest surprise of your life.

There is a rule in money management that you need to stick to no matter what. That rule is:

"Never risk more than 2% of your trading capital on any trade idea."

So, if you are trading a $10,000 account, make sure you risk no more than $200 on any trade. If you hold a $1,000 account, risk no more than $20 per trade.

Ideally, in the Forex market, this means that if you trade a $10,000 account, you should only trade no more than 1 or 2 standard lots per trade. At the same time, if you hold a $1,000 account, your risk should be no more than 1 or 2 mini lots per trade.

Again, always do the math by looking at the difference between your order entry price and the stop-loss order price to confirm this fact. If this isn't the case, either have the discipline to let the trade pass or reduce the lot size before you trade.

If you do so, you will be operating on what we call the "margin of safety" as you trade. This habit will keep you alive through the good and bad times that always inevitably occur in the business of trading.

We all desire to make a lot of money very quickly but unfortunately, this is one of the main reasons why many traders fail.

After you have read this book and you start implementing the techniques taught in here, you will inevitably taste some success. You may even hit a ten out of ten score the very first month you start. It happens. But that initial success may end up ruining a successful venture if you are not careful.

One of the many traps that you as a trader may fall into after you hit a long winning streak is that of dramatically increasing your position size. You may start thinking of how you can turn a $1,000 account into a $20,000 account. Don't do it.

Remember as I said before; increasing effective leverage may amplify profits on paper but it may also amplify the losses as well.

As a rule, you will lose by the same amount you stood to win. You may increase your position size so that you make $2,000 on a certain trade. However, if you weren't right, you may lose $1,000 or more in case you broke the rule on proper risk-reward ratios.

If that happens, you will not only lose the profits you had painfully accumulated through your previous winning trades, but also a significant portion of your trading capital. You could even receive a margin call or be wiped out completely. It has happened before to many traders who have tried this approach.

After this happens to you, you could hit a downward spiral that makes you even lose appetite for the trading business completely. So beware.

6. Avoid taking the same position in correlated instruments

Trading correlated or similar instruments or assets is another mistake that could significantly increase the overall risk in your portfolio.

As you begin practicing to trade, you will inevitably come across securities or assets that are essentially behaving in the same way. For instance, if one is trading upwards, the other one is doing the same. If one is stuck in a range, so is the other one. If you run into such a scenario, you need to mark the two as correlated instruments.

Examples of related instruments include pairs such as AUD/USD and AUD/CAD in the Forex market, Lumber and Timber in the Commodities markets and Coca-Cola and Pepsi in the Stock market.

What bearing does this have on your trading?

In the event that you take the same position on each one of these instruments, then you will have significantly raised your risk level. The amount of risk you will have taken will be the combined sum of the two positions.

If say, you risk 2% on each position, then this is more less the same as risking 4% on a single trade, a cardinal sin in trading. It won't take long before your trading suffers drastically if you continue down this path.

A good rule of thumb is to take positions in different directions at any given time. If you place a buy order on one instrument, then go and find another unrelated instrument that is giving you a sell signal and short it. This way, you will have created a perfectly balanced scenario.

If you must trade similar instruments, then take different positions. If you go long on one, go short on the other one. This way, one trade acts as a hedge against the other. If one goes up and you had taken a short position in it, you will be compensated by the one you took a long position in.

7. Trade with money you can afford to lose

Lastly, make sure that you trade with money that you can afford to lose.

Trading is one of the riskiest businesses that you could ever go into in this world. In this business, if you aren't making money, then you are losing it. Therefore, it helps to keep this reality in perspective when you decide to risk your money in this business.

Unlike most businesses, where the risk of loss is somewhat manageable, in trading, the risk of losing all your life savings is real. Sadly, there have been stories of people who risked their life savings in the financial markets and lost all of it, only to take their lives. It is for this reason that I have chosen to term this point as a risk management tip.

Only put aside money from either regular savings, from your entertainment budget or some variation of that before investing it in the market. If the money you are holding right now, planning to invest in this business is very important to you, then don't trade.

I always find it helpful to ask myself, "If something goes wrong with this investment and I lose all the money, will I be okay mentally and physically?" If the answer is yes, then I go ahead and invest it. You should do the same.

I know the adrenaline rush of trading and making thousands of dollars in the markets perhaps millions is bugging you, but you need to contain it. Trading is very risky and whoever tells you than they can guarantee you quick success in this business are lying to you.

One of the most appalling comments you will ever come across is that the average couple will spend days if not weeks debating on whether or not they should buy a $1,000 fridge, yet they will put the same amount, perhaps more in a stock, after receiving a tip from their broker friend and even apologize for not having more.

You may have also been tempted to buy one of those black-box trading systems from internet marketing gurus, which promise to double your money every few months, perhaps weeks.

Make no mistake; there is no easy money in trading. To be a little clearer, there is no quick easy path to riches, especially in trading. It is the result of hard work, study, time, risk and a bit of luck among other time-tested principles.

The reason I am pointing this one out is because the lure of easy money is what drives many people into investing money they shouldn't have invested in the first place. Most people never take even the time to read a book such as this one because it sounds like too much work.

Only invest a small portion of the money you can risk to lose, in the beginning as you trade. Then after you taste some success and start having more confidence in yourself and your methods, you can start slowly building up your stake.

But don't be in a rush to borrow money from friends and relatives or from your bank to invest in the markets.

In conclusion, risk management is one of the most important facets when it comes to trading and should therefore be considered at all cost. After all, it's your hard earned money you will be investing. Unless you want to lose all of it in a flash, you need to pay attention to what has been discussed here. Apply these concepts in a demo trading account so that you can truly appreciate their importance before you can try them out in the real world.

CHAPTER 8:
MAINTAINING SWING TRADING MOMENTUM

One of the things you'll need to remember about swing trading momentum is that managing it well is more of a fine art than an exact science. To successfully manage your swing trading momentum, you'll need to learn how to manage your trading risks wisely, to be a very patient person, and master your emotions. Compared to day trading where all your positions are closed within a few trading hours, swing trading takes days, weeks, and even a couple of months to come full circle. Its longer time frame requires a different trading viewpoint.

The following are four important things you should do to maximize your swing trading momentum and consequently, profits.

Set and Forget

As mentioned earlier, you'll need a lot of patience to succeed at swing trading. You shouldn't be monitoring every price tick that happens all throughout the trading day. Once you take a long position, forget it. Just take a look at its price once a day or every other day. With swing trades, you'll need to let your chosen securities build their momentum so you can enjoy potentially high profits.

If you micro-monitor your swing trading positions, you'll put yourself in a position where you'll be strongly tempted to liquidate earlier than you need to. When you succumb to such temptations, you'll either minimize your trading profits or maximize your losses because you prematurely liquidated your position.

So, just set price alerts near your primary profit-taking and stop-loss target prices and forget it. Just take action when the alerts are triggered.

Ditch the Micro Time Frames

With swing trading, you must focus more on the longer time frames because they're less volatile and by doing so, you minimize your risks for "false triggers" or whiplashes that can make you take positions on securities whose prices are still on a decline. The shortest time frame you should consider is daily, nothing less. The longer your time frame, the lesser the false triggers and noise you'll encounter, and the more you can maintain your winning swing trading streak.

Moving Averages for Risk Management

The easiest and most objective way to see a security's true trend is through moving averages. As such, moving averages can be your best ally in managing your swing trading risks and find more profitable swing trading entry points.

Often times, financial securities that are enjoying momentum retreat to their moving averages, the most common of which are the 20 and 50-day moving averages, before proceeding with the next price movement. As such, moving averages can help you time your swing trades with fairly high accuracy and ease.

Don't Cash in on Your Profits in One Fell Swoop

Many financial securities that are on a strong price momentum can continue for weeks and months on end. But the challenge is it's impossible to predict exactly how long bullish momentums run for specific securities. There's always the risk of liquidating too early when a security's price continues to soar after closing a position and waiting too long that its price has fallen deep from its peak.

By taking partial profits or liquidating part of your swing trading positions on securities that are on a strong upward momentum, you can lock in on some of the profits once your chosen security has reached your target profit-taking level. Because there are still some left, you can lock in on more profits if the momentum continues. If the price happens to come down after that, your initial profits could compensate for the smaller profit or loss on the remaining position.

Money and risk involve in swing trading

At the point when utilized accurately, swing trading is a brilliant procedure utilized by numerous dealers crosswise over different markets. It isn't just utilized in the Forex advertise, yet it is an indispensable apparatus in prospects and value markets. Swing dealers take the abilities that they learn through specialized examination and can even parlay these aptitudes into different choices methodologies. The transient idea of swing trading separates it from that of the customary financial specialist. Financial specialists will in general have a more extended term time skyline and are not customarily influenced by momentary value changes. As usual, one must recall that swing trading is just a single system and ought to be used just when properly comprehended. Like any trading procedures, swing trading can be dangerous, and moderate methodology can transform into day trading techniques rapidly. In the event that you intend to utilize a swing trading technique, guarantee that you completely comprehend the dangers and build up a procedure that will probably enable you to produce greatest rate returns on your positions.

Distinguishing stocks and executing beneficial trading's

Every year, crowds of new dealers that don't have a clue how to make benefits trading on the financial trading come in huge numbers to take a stab at making a fast fortune yet end up regularly being significantly more unfortunate than when they initially started. In the event that you need to make exceptional yields and stay away from the shock of extensive misfortunes in the securities trading, at that point you should comprehend that specific basic achievement components are principal to elite in the trading the financial trading.

To start with, you should comprehend that value activity is the way to trading benefits. Value activity is the development of any security's cost and is outwardly spoken to on a value outline. The reason that it is indispensable to comprehend value activity is that cost uncovers where the patterns are so you can abuse them for benefit.

Regardless of whether cost goes up or down, bullish or bearish, your capacity to spot inclines in the financial trading is as to productive trading as water is to angle. Without the capacity to comprehend value activity, you will always be unable to recognize client drifts and, are just, dead in the water.

Next, recall the old trading saying "the pattern is your companion" and stays with great with those patterns. Patterns can be your closest companion as long as you make sure to trading the course of a stock or security. Else, they can be your most noticeably terrible adversary, and it is nearly ensured that you will endure a long arrangement of awful misfortunes on the off chance that you trading against the force of the market.

Know your exit before your entrance is the following component that you should comprehend at a profound fundamental level in the event that you need to increase outsized benefits from the financial trading. In the motion picture, "Ronin," with Robert Deniro, Deniro plays a covert CIA specialist going into a bar late around evening time after it has shut to meet his contact. Prior to entering, he goes to the back of the bar, finds the secondary passage, puts a weapon by the exit, and after that strolls around the front and enters. Afterward, he clarifies that he never comes a structure without know where the entryway is and how to get out. This is solid counsel for the secret covert agent as well as for the merchant too.

In the event that you're going to put a situation in any speculation, at that point you should realize when you will get out in case, you're regularly going to realize how to make benefits trading on the securities trading. This applies both to benefit taking and your leave methodology; on the off chance that a stock hits a benefit target, at that point take benefits with no of the psychological re-thinking or enthusiastic clashes of whether to sit back and watch on the off chance that it goes considerably further to support you or not (numerous brokers have transformed winning positions into losing positions by only overlooking their leave targets excessively long).

In like manner, if a position conflicts with you and you wind up assuming a misfortune, at that point you should not be reluctant to cut free that position since you're terrified of assuming a misfortune. Trading is based on little misfortunes while making immense benefits on out of control moves since you had the great sense to exit losing positions rapidly and ride the grand slam trading s to their fullest potential.

Figure out how to have an independent mind. You figure out how to think for yourself by placing in an opportunity to find out about value activity, how to adventure patterns for securities trading benefits, and realizing when to get out before you ever make a passage. Perhaps the main motivation for trading disappointment, if not the most critical reason, is that starting merchants come into the market without an arrangement or the preparation to fall back on in light of the fact that they do not have a comprehension of these center standards.

Recognizing Stock Market Pattern

A few people view financial trading as a way to procure income sans work. This isn't valid. Just individuals with a touch of good karma could have benefits in the event that it was that simple. Individuals engaged with trading stock have done some examination to make a benefit. Recognizing the patterns of the market is the way to achievement in the financial trading. In the event that you can distinguish the patterns in financial trading, you can comprehend the conduct of a stock dependent on its past exhibition.

One of the fundamental presumptions of stock promoting organizations is that the market has patterns: essential, optional (present moment) and mainstream patterns (long-term). In view of these patterns, showcase watchers foresee the estimation of offers. Merchants use examples to recognize benefit or misfortune.

The securities trading can be a positively trending business sector or a bear showcase. A positively trending business sector shows the nearness of a larger number of purchasers than venders. This prompts an expansion in the estimation of offers. Despite what might be expected, if the quantity of venders is more than the quantity of purchasers, the measure of offers falls. It is said to be a bear showcase.

To distinguish a pattern, you need data on two basic elements of the financial trading: cost and volume. The value informs you concerning the course of development in the market, and the sum says whether there is development in the securities trading. There are situations when the volume of a stock is high, as is its cost. This demonstrates an upward pattern. On account of high limit and minimal effort, it is a descending pattern. In view of this, you may choose whether to sell or buy stocks.

In the event that you see customary descending days, the market is showing a slow down or upswing. It is astute to put resources into stocks as costs will undoubtedly hop back. On the other hand, in the event that it has been a nonstop time of high rates, the market is showing lower costs later on. It is the correct time to exit from the stock.

Frequently, it happens that the stock costs are expanding or diminishing. This may resemble a change to you. In any case, in the event that you look at the volume and find that there is definitely not a significant volume increment or lessening, you ought not anticipate a distinction in the securities tradingyet. While contemplating patterns is a decent propensity in securities trading, it is important to watch out for false flag.

Stocks, which are high in volume, for instance, common assets, will in general influence the development of the market. You can watch out for activity in such stocks to recognize potential changes. A few internet trading organizations give outlines and pattern pointers on their sites. These apparatuses can be utilized to consider the patterns in financial trading.

Before we dig into distinguishing stock patterns, allows first characterize what a pattern is "a predominant propensity or tendency" or "a line of general bearing or development." "pattern" is likewise utilized as an action word and signifies "to grow a general way." The utilization of the word pattern about the financial tradingwould then imply that a stock that is inclining is a stock that is moving a general way.

Stocks just move in three distinct ways, they climb, they go down, or they move sideways. Stock patterns are regularly discussed as far as either a bullish pattern, which means the stock cost is expanding or a bearish pattern, which means the stock cost is diminishing. On the off chance that a stock's cost is essentially going neither up nor down, yet moving sideways, it may not be seen by some to be in a pattern. In fact, for example, stock is a sideways way. The sideways example is additionally generally alluded to as a "time of combination."

There is any number of approaches to distinguish stock patterns. Probably the most straightforward approaches to do this is to take a gander at a stock graph. Stock diagrams are pervasive and can be discovered everywhere throughout the Internet at such puts as Yahoo Finance or Google money. In case you're taking a gander at a stock outline and the latest cost is higher than the past rates the stock can be said to be in an upswing. On the other hand, in case you're taking a gander at a stock graph and the latest costs are lower than the past costs on the table then the stock is said to be in a downtrend.

We have quite recently perceived that it is so natural to distinguish stock patterns. There is a significant inquiry that is on the psyche of everybody hoping to recognize a pattern. That question is, "does this pattern have the solidarity to proceed?" You see, when you distinguish an example, it simply isn't sufficient to know which course the market has been going, however which heading the market is well on the way to go from here. This is the reason it is basic to decide the quality of any pattern. The explanation behind this is. In a perfect world, we would get in on a pattern that has great force, the kind of vitality that could convey the stock cost toward a path that will make us a brilliant benefit.

There a few different ways to quantify a pattern's quality or shortcoming. Numerous investigators depend on the trading volume as a pointer that the intensity of the example is either expanding, diminishing, or staying generally the equivalent.

So when you are thinking about your next stock trading doesn't just mull over what the pattern has been, however more significantly, if that pattern is probably going to proceed.

Distinguishing the Right Stock Market Trading System

Fruitful trading relies upon three factors: the dealer's brain science, the capacity to oversee cash, and a financial trading framework that is exceptionally viable. This article talks about the securities trading framework and how brokers, particularly the apprentices, can decide on a framework that is appropriate for his trading style.

Simply ask the expert brokers who have turned out to be fruitful in this field throughout the years. They have a trading framework that produces winning stocks. They won't be the place they are currently if their financial trading framework does not work for them.

No two dealers are similar. In this manner a trading arrangement of one doesn't really imply that it will work a similar route for another. A few brokers put resources into their qualities while others deal with their shortcomings. A few frameworks plan to buy the estimation of the stock in the long haul. Others focus on the transient expense. The trading framework relies upon the brain research of the merchant too.

There are approaches to benefit from the financial trading framework, however there is one component that a dealer must need to succeed. They must be methodical. This implies the trading framework that works for them ought to be something they stay with all through their trading vocation, regardless of what occurs. The financial trading framework develops however the methodologies that they detailed dependent on the experience and the exercises that they gained from the mix-ups they unintentionally made can be their mystery to pick up the speculations they have as a primary concern. To put it plainly, merchants choose dependent on their methodologies and not their feelings.

Another mystery is to thought of a framework that fits the dealer's character. It resembles a couple of pants. It's difficult to look for the correct pair of pants on the grounds that the fit is fundamental. It resembles the securitiestrading framework for dealers. They should create one that they are alright with and can give them the outcomes that they need, in light of how they see themselves in their trading vocation.

Along these lines, the securities trading framework must be from a system which expands the qualities and limits the shortcomings of brokers. The present circumstance of the market should likewise be considered. Once in a while, dealers need capital development or income with the goal that their salary from trading can be made into benefits they can live on. On the off chance that dealers are certain about their aptitudes and have enough money to contribute, at that point they can continue with ongoing trading.

CHAPTER 9:
TREND PREDICTION

There are various procedures you can use to swing-exchange stocks. In the model demonstrated above, a swing exchange dependent on exchanging sign delivered utilizing a Fibonacci retracement. The three most significant focuses on the diagram utilized in this model incorporate the exchange passage point (i), leave level (iii) and stop misfortune (ii). Any swing exchanging framework ought to incorporate these three key components.

The stop misfortune level and leave point do not need to stay at a set value level as they will be activated when a specific specialized set-up happens, and this will rely upon the kind of swing exchanging technique you are utilizing. The assessed time span for this stock swing exchange is around multi week. It is imperative to know about the ordinary time allotment that swing exchanges unfurl over so you can adequately screen your exchanges and boost the potential for your exchanges to be gainful.

There are five swing trade methodologies beneath that you can use to recognize exchanging openings and deal with your exchanges from beginning to end. Apply these swing exchanging methods to the stocks you are most intrigued by to search for conceivable exchange section focuses. You can likewise utilize instruments, for example, CMC Markets' example acknowledgment scanner to enable you to recognize stocks that are appearing specialized exchanging signals.

Channel exchanging

This swing exchanging system necessitates that you recognize a stock that is showing a solid pattern and is exchanging inside a channel. On the off chance that you have plotted a channel around a bearish pattern on a stock diagram, you would consider opening a sell position when the value skips down off the top line of the channel. When utilizing channels to swing-exchange stocks it is imperative to exchange with the pattern, so in this model where cost is in a downtrend, you would search for sell positions – except if value breaks out of the channel, moving higher and demonstrating an inversion and the start of an upswing.

Fibonacci retracement

The Fibonacci retracement example can be utilized to enable brokers to recognize backing and opposition levels, and hence conceivable inversion levels on stock outlines. Stocks frequently will in general remember a specific rate inside a pattern before turning around once more, and plotting flat lines at the exemplary Fibonacci proportions of 35%, 46% and 70% on a stock diagram can uncover potential inversion levels. Merchants regularly take a gander at the half level also, despite the fact that it doesn't fit the Fibonacci design, since stocks will in general switch in the wake of remembering half of the past move.

A stock swing merchant could enter a momentary sell position if cost in a downtrend follows to and skips off the 70% retracement level going about as an obstruction level, with the mean to leave the sell position at a benefit when cost drops down to and bobs off the 35% Fibonacci line going about as a help level.

MACD hybrid

The MACD hybrid swing exchanging framework gives a basic method to distinguish chances to swing-exchange stocks. It is a standout amongst the most well known swing exchanging pointers used to decide pattern heading and inversions. The MACD comprises of two moving midpoints – the MACD line and sign line – and purchase and sell sign are created when these two lines cross. On the off chance that the MACD line crosses over the sign line a bullish pattern is demonstrated and you would consider entering a purchase exchange.

On the off chance that the MACD line crosses underneath the sign line a bearish pattern is likely, proposing a sell exchange. A stock swing merchant would then trust that the two lines will cross once more, making a sign for an exchange the other way, before they leave the exchange. The MACD wavers around a zero line and exchange sign are additionally created when the MACD crosses over the zero line (purchase signal) or underneath it (sell signal).

Support and obstruction triggers

Backing and obstruction lines speak to the foundation of specialized examination and you can assemble a fruitful stock swing exchanging system around them.

A help level demonstrates a value level or territory on the outline beneath the present market cost where purchasing is sufficiently able to conquer selling weight. Therefore, a decrease in cost is stopped and value turns back up once more. A stock swing merchant would hope to enter a purchase exchange on the ricochet off the help line, setting a stop misfortune underneath the help line.

Obstruction is something contrary to help. It speaks to a value level or territory over the present market cost where selling weight may beat purchasing weight, making the value turn down against an upswing. For this situation a swing dealer could enter an auction position on the skip the opposition level, setting a stop misfortune over the obstruction line. A key thing to recall with regards to fusing backing and opposition into your swing exchanging framework is that when value ruptures a help or obstruction level, they switch jobs – what was before a help turns into an opposition, and the other way around.

10-and 20-day SMA

One more of the most famous swing exchanging strategies includes the utilization of simple moving averages (SMAs).

SMAs smooth out value information by computing an always refreshing normal value which can be assumed control over a scope of explicit timeframes, or lengths. For instance, a 10-day SMA includes the day by day shutting costs throughout the previous 10 days and partitions by 10 to ascertain another normal every day. Each average is associated with the next to make a smooth line which removes the 'commotion' on a stock diagram. The length utilized, 10 for this situation, can be connected to any graph interim, from one moment to week by week. SMAs with short lengths respond more rapidly to value changes than those with longer time allotments.

With the 10-and 20-day SMA swing exchanging framework you apply two SMAs of these lengths to your stock diagram. At the point when the shorter SMA (10) crosses over the more SMA (20) a purchase sign is produced as this demonstrates an upswing is in progress. At the point when the shorter SMA crosses beneath the more drawn out term SMA, a sell sign is created as this sort of SMA hybrid shows a downtrend.

These techniques can be connected to your trading to enable you to recognize exchanging openings the business sectors you are most intrigued by. The propelled diagrams are outfitted with every one of the five of the pointers and attracting devices required to incorporate the above procedures, in addition to numerous other specialized markers and studies.

The Best Swing Trading Indicators

Indicators are augmentations on the outline that give additional data through scientific estimations on volume and cost. Additionally, they disclose to you where the cost is probably heading straightaway.

Specialized trading includes looking into graphs and settling on choices dependent on examples and pointers. These examples are specific shapes that candles structure on an outline, and can give you data about where the cost is probably going to go straightaway.

There are 4 noteworthy indicators that you shoul consider as a swing trader: momentum, trend, volatility and volume.

Momentum indicators disclose to you how solid the pattern is and can likewise let you know whether an inversion will happen. They can be valuable for choosing value tops and bottoms. Momentum markers incorporate the Ichimoku Kinko Hyo, the Relative Strength Index, the Average Directional Index and the Stochastic.

Trend indicators disclose to you which course the market is moving in, if there is a pattern by any stretch of the imagination. They are now and again called oscillators, since they will in general move among high and low qualities like a wave. Trend markers incorporate the Parabolic SAR, the Moving Average Convergence Divergence and the Ichimoku Kinko Hyo.

Volatility indicators reveal to you the extent the cost is varying over a stretch of time. Unpredictability is a significant piece of the market, making it very difficult to profit when it is not there. The cost needs to move for you to make a benefit.

Volume indicators reveal to you the extent volume is shifting after a while, what number of pieces of bitcoin that are purchased and sold during the long haul. This is helpful on the grounds that when the value is altered, the volume shows how solid the move is. Bullish proceeds on high volume are bound to be kept up than those when the volume is low.

The higher the instability is, the quicker a cost is evolving. It reveals to you nothing about bearing, only the scope of costs.

Low instability shows little value moves, high unpredictability demonstrates huge value moves. High instability additionally recommends that there are value wasteful aspects in the market, and merchants refer to wastefulness as profit.

So for what reason are markers so significant? Indeed, they give you a thought of where the cost may go next in a given market. Toward the day's end, this is the thing that we need to be familiar with as dealers. Where is the value moving towards in order to be position ourselves to exploit the move and profit.

When you choose to be a dealer, you must comprehend where the market may move towards, and be set up for any projection. You do not have to figure out precisely where the market will go, yet comprehend the various conceivable outcomes, and be situated for whichever one appears.

Keep in mind, merchants make cash in bear and markets. It is important to exploit short and long positions. Try not to get excessively appended to the bearing of the market, provided the cost is in motion, you can benefit. Pointers will assist you in this case.

The following are the important swing trading indicators that will make all the difference for you;

Ichimoku Kinko Hyo (Ichimoku Cloud)

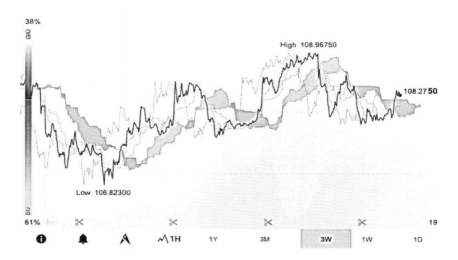

This is an accumulation of lines plotted on a chart. It is a pointer that estimates future value force, and decides territories of future help and opposition. At first look this resembles an exceptionally unpredictable marker, so it is necessary to understand them in detail;

Tenkan Sen (red line): This is the turning line that is determined by averaging the most astounding high and the least low for as far back as nine periods.

Senkou Span: This is the first Senkou line that is determined by

226

getting the mean of the Kijun Sen as well as the the Tenkan Sen then plotting the 26 periods in front. The second Senkou line is determined by finding the mean of the most elevated high then the least low in the course of the last 52 periods. Thereafter, it is plotted 26 periods ahead.

Kijun Sen (blue line): Also referred to as the standard line, this is determined by finding the mean of the most noteworthy high then the least low for as far back as 26 periods on the chart.

Chikou Span: Also called the slacking line. It is the present shutting cost plotted 26 periods behind.

So how might you make an interpretation of these lines into exchanging benefits?

The Senkou length goes about as powerful help and opposition levels. In the event that the cost is over the Senkou range, the top line goes about as the primary help, and the primary concern being the secondary help.

On the off chance that the costs beneath the Senkou length, the primary concern goes about as the principal opposition, and the top line as the subsequent obstruction.

The Kijun Sen (the blue line) is utilized to affirm patterns. On the off chance that the value breakouts over the Kijun Sen, it's probably going to increase more. Alternately, on the off chance that the value dips under this line, at that point it is probable that it will go lower.

The Tenkan Sen (red line) can likewise be utilized to affirm patterns. On the off chance that the line is going up or down, it shows the market is slanting. Also, on the off chance that it is moving sideways, at that point the market is extending. Keep in mind, the line is a pattern pointer.

The Chikou range is about 26 periods following the present time frame. This is an important reality to recollect. It very well may be utilized as a pattern marker of all types. At the point when the line passes the cost in a base up heading, the cost is probably going to go up. At the point when the line passes the cost in a up-down course, the cost is probably going to decrease.

That is a ton going on in one pointer. Furthermore, a mess of data it can give you. You simply need to recollect what each line implies. On the off chance that you get the Chikou Span and the Kijun Sen stirred up, at that point you can easily confuse a trend that is downward with an upswing. What's more, that would be shocking for your exchanging account.

Bollinger Bands

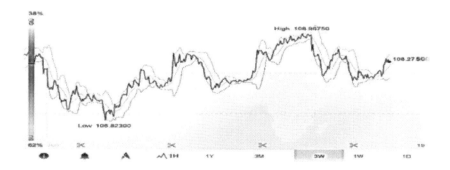

Bollinger groups are an unpredictability pointer. They comprise of a straightforward moving normal, and two lines placed at two standard deviations on each part of the focal moving normal line. Additionally, the external lines build the band.

Essentially, if the band is restricted the market is tranquil. At the point when the band is wide the market is boisterous. It is possible to utilize Bollinger Bands in exchanging both running and drifting markets.

Within a running business sector, pay special mind to the Bollinger Bounce. The value will in general skip from one side of the band to the next, continually coming back to the normal in motion. It is possible to comprehend this as relapse to the mean. Therefore, the value normally comes back to the normal over the long haul.

In this circumstance, the groups go about as powerful help and obstruction levels. In the event that the value hits the highest point of the band, at that point put in a sell request that has a stop misfortune simply over the band to secure from any break outs. The cost ought to return down towards the normal, and possibly to the base band, where you could take benefits. Look at the screen capture underneath.

At the point during the market incline, it is possible to utilize the Bollinger Squeeze to know when to exchange section and get the breakouts at an opportune time. At the point when the groups draw nearer together, for example they crush, it demonstrates that a breakout is going to occur. It does not disclose to you anything about bearing so be set up at the cost to go in any case.

On the off chance that the candles breakout underneath the base band, this will for the most part proceed in a downtrend. On the off chance that the candles breakout over the band at the top, this will by and large proceed in an upturn. Investigate the screen capture underneath.

In rundown, pay special mind to the Bollinger Bounce in running markets, the cost will in general come back to the mean. In inclining markets, utilize the Bollinger Squeeze. It does not disclose to you what direction the cost will go, only that it will go.

Parabolic Stop and Reverse (SAR)

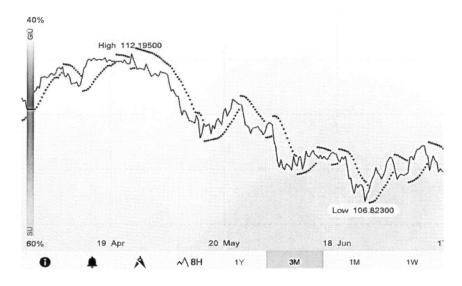

This is a pattern marker. Specks are put on the graph above or beneath the cost, and they demonstrate the potential heading of the value development. By what means can such a straightforward pointer be utilized in exchanging? At the point when the dabs are over the value, the market is in downtrend, demonstrating that you ought to be short.

At the point when the dabs are beneath the value, the market is in an upswing, showing that you ought to be long. Try not to utilize Parabolic SAR in an extending market at a time when the cost is moving from side to side. At present will be a great deal of commotion and the specks will switch from one side to another, making you not doubt the reasonable sign.

Include the Parabolic SAR to your exchanging arms stockpile and utilize it to understand solid patterns.

Relative Strength Index (RSI)

This is an energy pointer plotted on a different scale. There is a solitary line measured from zero to one hundred that recognizes conditions that are sold or bought too frequently in the market. When it is more than 70 demonstrate an market characterized by overbought conditions, and when it is underneath 30 show an oversold showcase.

The entire thought of RSI is to select both bottom and top to make it in a market when the pattern is turning around. This will assist you with taking bit of leeway of the entire time. Investigate the graph beneath.

RSI can likewise be utilized to affirm pattern developments. In the event that RSI is over the 50 mark, then the market is most likely in an upswing. Then again, when the line is underneath 50, then the market is presumably in a downtrend.

On the off chance that you are more risk averse, at that point hanging tight for pattern affirmation might be the best approach. It is an exchange off between 2 things. You can remain to make more benefit by familiarizing yourself with a pattern early, yet you will additionally not be right more regularly and possibly drop a bunches of pips to the stops.

Then again you can trust that the pattern will be affirmed and be correct all the more regularly, however you will likewise miss a bit of the move so remain to make less benefit.

Everything relies upon your hazard manner. Is it true that you will acknowledge numerous little misfortunes and a couple of huge champs? Or on the other hand do you need bunches of littler victors?

Moving Average Convergence Divergence (MACD)

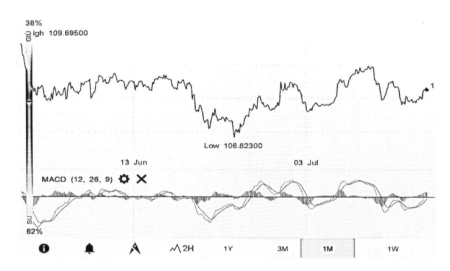

This is a pattern pointer and it comprises of a quick line, moderate line, as well as a histogram. The contributions for this pointer are a number characterizing the period for one more moving normal (MA-period), a quicker moving normal (MA-quick) and a slower-moving normal (MA-moderate).

The MACD quick line is a normal of the distinction comparing MA-quick and the MA-moderate. Give. The MACD moderate line is a normal that is moving of the MACD quick line. The quantity of time is characterized by MA-period.

The MACD is that it is comprised of moving midpoints of other moving midpoints. This implies it lingers behind cost a considerable amount, so probably will be the worse of the markers to utilize on the off chance that you need to get into patterns early. Yet, it is extraordinary for affirming patterns.

Average Directional Index

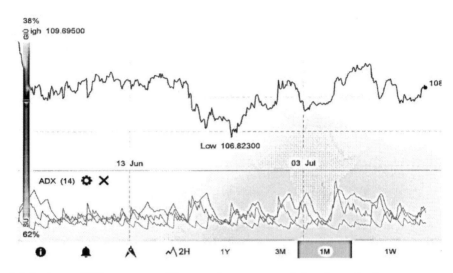

This is a different oscillator, however, this time it is a pattern marker. Average Directional Index (ADX) figures run from zero to one hundred and are expected to let you in on a sign of pattern quality.

On the off chance that ADX is underneath 20, the pattern is frail. On the off chance that it is over 50, the pattern is solid. Remember however, that ADX does not disclose to you the bearing of the pattern, only the quality.

When exchanging, you can utilize ADX to maintain a strategic distance from fallouts. It is truly best utilized in mix with different markers, as, in spite of the name, it does not give you any data about pattern bearing.

Joined with a directional pattern pointer, for example, Parabolic SAR, ADX will affirm that a pattern is solid and will proceed. This will accord you greater certainty when going into a position.

ADX over fifty is a solid pattern. ADX can likewise assist you with exiting the trade when the pattern debilitates to abstain from getting captured by value retracements.

Similarly, as with many pattern pointers, ADX lingers behind the cost, so isn't valuable on the off chance that you need to get in on patterns early. Be that as it may, it is helpful on the off chance that you just need to exchange solid patterns.

Stochastic

This is an energy pointer, and can be utilized to discover where a pattern may end. Along these lines to RSI, it is utilized to decide when a benefit is oversold or overbought.

It is comprised of 2 lines on another diagram. If you have just speculated, stochastic will assist you with picking a section point and get into a pattern at the absolute starting point. At the point when the stochastic lines are over 80, it shows an overbought market and raises the possibility of a downtrend is probably going to pursue.

Presently when the stochastic lines are underneath 20, it demonstrates an oversold market, making an uptrend probable.

Indistinguishable provisos from RSI apply here. When attempting to get into patterns right on time, there will be numerous odds, so you ought to be set up with stop misfortunes on the off chance that the market does not go your direction. As usual, utilize the pointer to give you a thought of where the market is probably going to go.

These are 7 famous markers that you will see around when you start swing trading. Make your own diagrams, play around with the pointers and discover how they work. The default factors for the markers may be appropriate for cryptographic forms of money, or for an exchanging way to transform them. Perceive how the factors influence the sign from the markers, and if this makes better passages, or causes you to get improved patterns.

CHAPTER 10:
CANDLESTICKS AND BAR CHARTS

The method that most swing traders are going to rely on is technical analysis. This is based on the principle that past price movements in a security are going to be a predictor of how it will move in the future. Trading volume or the number of securities that are traded is often going to be combined together with the price movement to help you get better price prediction models overall.

In this chapter, we are just going to take a look at the basics of charting with a technical analysis. We are going to take a look at some of the different types of charts and chart patterns that you can look for when you want to do a swing trade to help you make the right decisions with your trade.

Some of the topics that we need to look into when we are learning how to chart with a technical analysis include the following:

- Candlesticks

- Bar charts

- Candlestick patterns

- Price action and psychology

Candlesticks

Candlesticks are not just going to represent the price action of the stock during that particular period of time. When you put a few of them together in a timeline, it can provide the trader with a window into some insight about the sentiment throughout the market for how others view the stock. Candlesticks are going to examine and show the majority of the traders' psyche regarding how much the stock is valued over the time that you are examining.

In order to create this kind of chart, you need to have a few different numbers present. The numbers that are the most important include:

- Beginning price for the chosen time frame (This number is also known as the opening price.)

- Highest price in that time frame

- The lowest price in that time frame

- The last price in that time frame or the closing price

You can choose how long you want the time frame to be. For example, you can do one minute, five minutes, hourly, daily, weekly, and more. Most swing traders are going to look at a daily chart or at a longer period of time because you will hold onto the security for a few days or even a few weeks, so these numbers help you out a bit more. But, when you use the set of four numbers above, you will be able to create a candlestick pattern.

The candlestick is going to have a body and then two tails. The wide portion of the candlestick is known as the body. Then, the long thin lines that show up both below and above the body will show the high and low-price range, and these are known as the tails, the wicks, or the shadows. The top of the upper tail will identify the higher price in that period, and the bottom of the lower tail will help to identify the lowest price in that period.

There are a lot of different scenarios that you are able to find when you are working with the candlestick pattern. If a stock ended up closing out that period at a high of that time frame, then you won't see a top tail because the high of that period was also the closing price. But, if a stock started out at the lowest price of that time period and then traded last at the highest price, then you would see no tails either on the top or the bottom of the body.

Sometimes, a single or a double candlestick can provide an indication of how the stock will move in the future. You can also take a look at how they are doing over several different time periods to get a good idea of how the stock is going to move in the future.

Bar Charts

Another option that you can use to monitor your stock prices includes bar chars. For this one, instead of going through and creating a body for each of the time frames that you are working with, you will see just a simple vertical line that will show the range of the price movement over whatever time period you are looking at. Then, on each side of the vertical line, there is also a small horizontal line.

On the left side, the small horizontal line will show the price at the start of your chosen time period, and then, the horizontal line on the right side will show the last price that stock was traded at when the time period ends. You can also add in some colors to the bar charts to help you visualize the way that the price is moving during that time.

No matter which type of chart that you are using, both of these can help you tell if a stock is a great deal about the general trend of a stock and the level of interest is there with the sellers and the buyers of the stock. This can help you make some great decisions when it comes to which stocks you would like to purchase with this method.

Price Action and Psychology

When you are looking at traders, they can all be separated out into three categories. These include the buyers, the sellers, and those who are undecided. As with any market, a buyer wants to enter into a trade paying as little as they possibly can, while the sellers want to be able to charge as much as they can. These different perspectives between the purchasers and sellers can cause a bid-ask spread. The actual prices of the transaction will be a result of the actions and the decisions of all the traders at that point in time, including the sellers, the buyers, and those who are undecided.

The presence and actions of undecided traders can put pressure on either the sellers or the buyers based on which way the undecided group is leaning. These undecided traders could then decide to take a position and make the deals that others are considering. If the buyers end up taking too long to decide on what to do, it is possible that someone else could do it first and will drive the prices up. In the same idea, the sellers who wait too long to get a higher price could be disappointed when others sell at a bid that would drive the prices down. Having an awareness of these undecided traders can help to ensure that the sellers and buyers are actually going to be willing to trade with each other.

The buyers will keep buying because they expect that, at some point, the prices are going to head up. If there are more buyers compared to sellers, then the result is that the buyers will pay a higher price in order to get the stock before other buyers do. They worry that, if they don't do it now or don't make the purchase, they are going to end up having to pay a much higher price later on.

When the undecided traders see that the price is increasing, they may also decide that they want to become buyers, which can add in a sense of urgency even more with all of the buyers. The price of the stock will then accelerate upwards even further than before.

On the other side of things are the sellers. These traders are selling because they think that the prices are going to start going down at some point. When the price is dropping, it means that the sellers are the ones in control now. The result is that the sellers will start to accept lower prices in order to get out of the position and at least make some profit. The worry for the sellers here is they think that, if they don't sell right away, they are going to miss out on profits and will have to sell at an even lower price.

When it comes to the undecided traders who are holding onto the stock, when they see that the pressure for selling is happening, they are going to start selling as well. This added selling from these traders is going to start creating a bigger sense of urgency among the sellers, which can cause the price of the stock to drop even faster.

Your goal, as the swing trader, is to find the balance of power that occurs between the sellers and the buyers, and then, you will go in and bet on the group you think will win. The candlestick charts are going to be a good way to see the sentiment of the majority of the traders and investors during a specific time period. A successful trader is able to use their tools to help them interpret the sentiment towards a stock, so they can make smart decisions on how to purchase and sell stocks.

CHAPTER 11:
SWING TRADING RULES FOR SUCCESS

Swing exchanging for amateurs is an incredible method to profit for tenderfoot dealers it's straightforward and learns, and if you pursue the 4 Rules here, you will be well on your approach to swing exchanging achievement.

Swing exchanging is a technique for transferring that depends on getting responses within real patterns either up or down, and for the most part, a swing exchange will last between 2 - 5 days. Some forex brokers attempt and swing trade within daily time outline; however, this is a catastrophe waiting to happen; it doesn't work, so don't try it.

Here are your four principles to pursue accomplishment in swing exchanging

Rule 1: Use Support and Resistance

When you swing exchange forex, you should spot territories of help and obstruction on the daily forex graph. In a perfect world, ones that have seen costs spike on high unpredictability are great as these tend not to last so utilize the Bollinger band just as pattern lines. For the most part, the more trial of obstruction there is the more substantial it is so 3 x tests or more and two diverse time casings is perfect. When swing exchanging forex DON'T commit this standard error:

Numerous dealers trust that the cost will draw near to the dimension there taking a gander at and essentially enter an exchanging sign and expectation the aspect holds - This will prompt a quick crash don't trust or foresee your speculating, and the business sectors won't reward you, they will take your value.

You must get the chances on your side, and for this, you have to watch value force.

Rule 2: Watch Momentum

For instance, when costs approach a dimension sit tight for value energy to turn back as estimated by force oscillators. When you are swing exchanging forex or some other money-related instrument, this affirms your exchanging signal. We don't have enough space to cover the individual markers here. However, you should begin with the stochastic and Relative Strength Index (RSI).

Presently you're in the exchange the following guideline includes the import yet making a few benefits!

Rule 3: Set a Target

When you enter a swing, exchange benefits and misfortunes ten to come rapidly, the stop is anything but difficult to put and self-evident - behind the help or obstruction, you are taking a gander at. When you can utilize a stop close premise. Set an objective just before where you think the cost will proceed to take it early.

Remember, you can hold tight; however, the chances of progress will diminish as you get to the objective dimension so better to take care of it right off the bat in the event of a response. Albeit a few exchanges will keep running on the chances will be to support you more by banking early. So, there you have it a straightforward swing exchanging framework that is perfect for swing exchanging for novices and will work for any broker. You may state that is excessively straightforward - however, the best frameworks are, and necessary structures beat entangled ones, as there are fewer components to break.

Rule 4: Shop Spreads

You should exchange unstable, fluid monetary standards when swing exchanging. In the majors, you ought to have the option to get some tight spreads of only a few pips. All dealers are not risen to with regards to spreads, pick carefully, as exchange costs mount up and you must get the most secure ranges you can. Swing exchanging for learners is a perfect type of trading. It's easy to learn and can be an incredible expansion to your forex exchanging procedure and make healthy long-term gains, whether done accurately and help you appreciate cash exchanging achievement.

Take Profits Using Futures Swing Trading

Brief Time Frame Trading

Fates swing exchanging is taking another prospect's position and shutting a similar position within a fixed length of time. The exchanges generally last a couple of hours or a couple of days. The principal target is to ride on momentary pricing patterns until pricing depletion. Any monetary instruments, for example, wares, stock lists, values, or bonds, tends to move in a specific heading for a medium or long-term period.

Meaning of Swing Trading

There are numerous books on swing exchanging, and much has been composed on it. It is a targeted strategy for evaluating any money related instrument's value development. Trading on value patterns gives an unpleasant sign of what a prospects contract is probably going to do, and this catches the market instability on that fates contract cost.

Without utilizing swing exchanging, it is almost unthinkable or even hard to foresee prospects value developments. This is because passionate and coherent variances move budgetary markets. The enthusiastic part of the here and their events is hard to measure. Frequently there is an incredible effect and different times little result. Fortunately, swing exchanging procedures can support us.

Investigating Short-Term Trends

We can watch short term value patterns utilizing pattern analysis. Trend investigation demonstrates how a money-related instrument has moved in the past using relapse device to catch the possible future value development of the prospects contract.

Moving Averages Regression Line

A relapse line could be drawn dependent on past value developments. Any budgetary instrument with quick events underneath or more the relapse line has a high instability. High unpredictability is helpful for the broker who is hoping to purchase or shorting. Start by estimating the past presentation of the money related instrument. You would then be able to utilize it to foresee execution later.

When you have rudimentary comprehension of how a prospects contract cost moved previously, you can start to break down how it will move later. A moving normal is an average cost over a fixed measure of time. You can set it to 3 days, seven days, 50 days. Commonly, a multi-day moving average is being utilized by expert brokers as a relapse line. When the cost wanders from the relapse line, it is probably going to return to the front, as it might have obstruction or backing above and underneath the relapse line. At the point when the cost separates from the relapse line drastically, you can benefit from the unpredictable swings, and this is called swing exchanging.

Prospects swing exchanging is exchanging fates contracts for a foreordained term. As prospects exchanging includes high influence, it allows you to benefit extraordinarily from the unstable value swings. Regularly, you foresee where the cost of a prospects contract will go later, from where it is today. Going into a prospects contract on an enormous swing in value hence permits a significant section cost for the fates contract. This is how you can utilize swing exchanges to benefit.

Anticipating stock, record and future costs aren't troublesome, yet they do rely upon small scale and large-scale level money related and financial issues. There are no sacred goal techniques that can enable you to make 100% beneficial exchanges. Swing exchanging encourages you in figuring out where the prospects markets will head later and furthermore whether the fates markets members have adequately evaluated the fates contracts you are trading.

CHAPTER 12:
RISK MANAGEMENT

To be an active securities exchange broker, you should pursue a risk the executive's plan. A chance the executive's plan helps safeguard trading capital while procuring reliable returns. It likewise helps control your feelings while implementing self-restraint. The primary components of risk the board incorporate deciding the risk sum and position estimate, distinguishing the stop price, and looking at the risk/remunerate proportion.

Decide the Risk Amount

The risk sum is the most extreme sum you are happy to risk on some random exchange. It is typically a set level of your all-out record esteem. A typical principle guideline is to risk 1-3% of your complete record an incentive with each exchange. This sum ought to be diminished in times of high instability. In this way, a dealer with a capital of $50,000 that risks 2% per exchange would risk $1000 on each transaction.

Distinguish Stop Price

Before entering an exchange, you should set a stop misfortune price to help limit misfortunes and the impact of feelings. This price speaks to the dimension at which your position will be shut if the exchange moves against you. It will be activated consequently when the stock price exchanges at or past that dimension. Remember that slippage may happen, and you may lose more than you had at first determined. A stop misfortune request ensures execution; however, the price may move further against you before the exchange is executed.

Figure Position Size

When you have decided the risk sum and stop price, you would then be able to ascertain several offers that you will exchange. This number, or position estimate, can be determined by partitioning the risk sum by the risk-per-share. The risk-per-share is the distinction between the stop price and the entry price. In this way, expect your most extreme risk sum is $1000 per exchange. If your entry price is $30 and your stop misfortune price is $28, at that point, the risk-per-offer would be $2. To ascertain the position estimate, straightforward separation $1000 by $2. Your position size would be 500 offers.

Entry price $30 - Stop price $28 = $2 Risk-per-share

$1,000/$2 = 500 offers

Look at Risk/Reward

Looking at the risk/remunerate proportion is critical in deciding if a sensible benefit potential exists concerning the risk. It is an essential part of your general money the executive's procedure. The reward-per-share is the contrast between the actual price and the entry price. The risk-per-share is the distinction between the entry price and the stop price. The risk/remunerate proportion ought to be set up before entering an exchange and ought to never be under 1:3. All together words, the benefit an incentive for each exchange arrangement must be in any event multiple times bigger than the risk esteem. When your entry price is $30, and your actual cost is $36, at that point the reward-per-offer would be $6. With a stop loss of $28, your risk/compensate proportion would be 2:6, or 1:3.

- Entry price $30 - Stop price $28 = $2 Risk-per-share

- Target price $36 - Entry price $30 = $6 Reward-per-share

- 2:6 = 1:3 Risk Reward Ratio

More Money Management Tips

For online day trading, just exchange stocks that have an average trading volume of more than 1,000,000 offers for the day. For swing trading, only exchange stocks that have an average trading volume of more than 300,000 suggestions for every day. Likewise, you should exchange stocks that are priced above $5. Specialized investigation may bomb on stocks underneath this price since they can be effectively controlled.

Synopsis

Understanding and following appropriate stock trading risk, the board rules will enable you to limit your misfortunes while acquiring steady returns. Carefully monitoring your money, the board standards will help keep the feeling out of the exchange.

Manual for Swing Trading Strategy

The swing trading system is regularly used to win benefits from transient price changes in the securities exchange. It is generally known as a successful system to expand benefits while acquiring insignificant risks and misfortunes. Picking the correct stock and the right market assumes an essential job in the swing trading system. Swing merchants generally choose stocks with outrageous vacillations. This trading procedure is usually executed if the market is steady. The steadiness of the market results to minor varieties in the cash price, which can be useful to swing brokers. The procedure isn't pertinent if the market is quickly rising or slamming.

Since it includes a shorter course of events and fewer risks, the swing day procedure is prevalent among dealers who are yet working their way in the outside cash advertise.

Trading in supplies of large organizations can result in higher benefits in a shorter span. Selling of these significant stocks, otherwise called enormous top stocks, as a rule, happens in stock trades. Taller varieties can be found in their prices contrasted with different stocks, along these lines inferring increment in benefits for the swing brokers. As a rule, a swing broker adheres to a specific stock as it increments in worth, however, may move to another capital if the pattern changes. Along these lines, a swing trading methodology would possibly be fruitful if the correct stock has been picked.

For a swing trading procedure to guarantee achievement and benefits for the swing broker, the decision of the market is likewise an essential factor. The development of the stock prices in a market with a rising or falling pattern takes a solitary course. This single course of evolution would prompt lesser gainful varieties for the swing broker. Steady demand is progressively fitting for swing brokers where its fall promptly trails the ascent of the record.

There are confinements to the arrangements you can take before the exchange. A level of risk shirking is additionally engaged with the procedure. In trading, you will, in the long run, become familiar with the art through a genuine encounter and presentation to risks and misfortunes. Swing merchants additionally utilize various methodologies and pursue alternate points of view. Consequently, the average return in swing trading enormously differs. Using a segment of the capital is a smart thought to oversee risks for the individuals who have just been in the field for a long while. However, it doesn't remain constant for the newcomers and amateurs. Taking positions that are more noteworthy than what your resistance for risk can deal with would be inconvenient to your presentation. Swing merchants should concentrate their endeavors and focus on producing the development of the price. In like manner, you ought to likewise be inspired to be a superior broker since that would involve more money coming in. New swing dealers are additionally not encouraged to put in a lot of money in their record for their underlying exchanges. It can bring a newcomer a higher number of misfortunes than additions. At the underlying stage, the most magnificent suggested capital is $35,000.00.

Risk Management - Stock Market

Numerous individuals ignore the significance of overseeing risk in their positions and exchanges. As a trader or financial specialist, this is the main thing that we can control. We can't control the bearings of the markets. We likewise can't control whether we will win or lose in any position we take. The main thing inside our control is the measure of misfortune we will endure.

To most traders, risk management implies essentially setting stops. Numerous financial specialists don't do this to control risk. In any case, there is considerably more to deal with your risk in the markets. You wouldn't drive onto an extension if you have seen that the more significant part of the backings has disintegrated, would you? OK walk onto a solidified lake in the wake of seeing a "Slim Ice" sign posted and a few breaks appearing in the ice itself? You wouldn't, that is because you watched the earth and understood that it was too risky to even think about proceeding.

We must watch a similar order when we are engaged with the money related markets. To dissect risk before exchanging or contributing, we should take a gander at the present market condition, the security's, and the pattern. Is it safe to say that we are in a risk recognize that would block us from taking an exchange? Assume the markets were bearish, your security has quite recently discharged frustrating profit and is close supply on your exchanging time frame. OK purchase shares since costs climbed somewhat? Likely, you wouldn't. Even though you have a momentary bullish move, the staggering bearishness of the markets discloses to you that the earth is risky and the reward isn't huge enough to embrace an extended position.

Numerous individuals can design an exchange, however, not all be able to break down the risk and deal with the threat in a way that guarantees their money-related survival in the markets when things turn out badly. Also, trust me, they will now and then.

There are three main risk management methods that I wish to examine here:

Recurrence

In exchanging and contributing, recurrence alludes to the number of positions we will open. The issue with numerous traders/speculators is that they will attempt to accept every single open entryway they see and public areas with just a minimal possibility for progress. They do this because of the dread of passing up on chances and profits in the markets.

Successful traders/speculators have the order to be increasingly particular in their opening of positions and take just those exchanges that meet explicit criteria laid out in their arrangement and that offer a high likelihood for profits. As another trader/financial specialist, you should constrain the number of exchanges you take. This will compel you to search for the correct chances to exchange as opposed to bouncing in on any little move in the markets. Keep in mind, regardless of whether you pass up on an opportunity; there is likely another tagging along very soon.

Duration

The following method is duration, or the measure of time spent in the position. The more you pay in an area, the higher the shot for unfavorable value development. This is the reason speculators go out on a limb in the markets than traders do. When we center around littler time frame diagrams, we have less profit potential yet besides, significantly less risk. Exchanging on littler time frames decreases the threat we face in our exchanges.

This does not imply that we ought not to hope to profit from longer time frame positions. You can make up for the expanded duration risk by diminishing the other two elements of size or potentially recurrence. Longer term traders and financial specialists can, in any case, oversee risk well.

The duration may likewise be turned down when instability in the markets rise. Rising uncertainty causes increasingly extraordinary cost swings. As another trader who is not used to exchanging these swings, you are best served by lessening your presentation to them by exchanging littler time frames

Volume

Volume is the most significant viewpoint to your risk management plan. Tweet: Volume is the most considerable angle to the risk management plan. Capacity for a trader/speculator is the offered size we are taking per position. A great many people need to profit; however much as could be expected, yet by taking a bigger offer size, we are additionally expanding our risks. Volume should begin as training, in a recreated record, with no cash at risk. After successfully rehearsing you may build your risk with negligible offers. If you continue progressing nicely, progressively increment your offer size.

The watchword in the last sentence is steady. Numerous traders feel they should go from 100 to 1000 offers or 1000 to 10000 offers. This builds your risk ten times! You are much improved off by close to multiplying your offer size or risk for each progression and possibly do as such when you are accomplishing a definite win/misfortune proportion. When you risk more cash in a situation, there is a mental impact that you will take note. Watching profits and misfortunes increment exponentially can unleash ruin on another trader's mind. This may make you frenzy and leave positions too early or to clutch failures as you become solidified with dread.

When you are not exchanging or contributing admirably whenever you ought to promptly analyze your risk management, the main thing is to diminish your volume (share estimate). Also, be increasingly specific in your positions and turn down the recurrence. In conclusion, you can likewise decrease the duration of exchanges to counterbalance instability.

Everybody has an alternate equalization of these risk management devices that they ought to utilize.

The courses at Online Trading Academy show you the best possible risk management. When you have finished them, you will work independently with your neighborhood focus' understudy bolster pro just as your instructive advisor to locate the correct equalization for your circumstance and to exchange plan.

The Best Forex Swing Trading Indicator

Is it safe to say that you are searching for an indicator to give you an edge in your swing trading? Maybe the most popular and generally utilized sort of symbol for swing trading, or any trading, are momentum oscillator indicators. There is a wide assortment of momentum oscillator indicators accessible, one of which is known as the stochastic indicator.

Momentum indicators are driving indicator. They guarantee to lead value development by offering to understand potential future value activity. Momentum indicators do this by estimating momentum, or by how much the cost of any instrument changes.

As a cash pair or stock increments in value, momentum indicators will ascend alongside value development. As their ascent starts to moderate the momentum indicator will begin to drop. This cautions of the back of or loss of momentum in the money pair or stock.

The stochastic indicator is a momentum-based indicator and offers to alarm brokers of when a money pair or stock might be overbought or oversold. At the point when an instrument is overbought or oversold, some sort of a pullback or change is typical. The stochastic indicators can caution of when these overbought and oversold levels might be conceivably come to, enabling dealers to either fix their stop misfortunes to abstain from giving back an excessive amount to the market or shutting their exchanges and taking their benefits before the market drops and deletes any gains they had open.

Momentum indicators are generally utilized by speculative stock investments, banking organizations and numerous enormous corporate swing trading organizations. A standout amongst the most prevalent is the stochastic indicator. At the point when utilized appropriately, you will know ahead of time when markets might reach overbought or oversold levels, allowing you to deal with your exchanges before it is past the point of no return.

What's the Best Swing Trading Indicator For You?

Finding the correct swing trading indicator can at some point be extremely troublesome. Specialized trading with indicators is conceivable, and numerous merchants around the globe can make benefits all day every day because of the understanding that trading indicators offer to those with the aptitudes to utilize them. When you are merely beginning, at that point, the issue is that there are numerous indicators accessible. This makes it incredibly troublesome when settling on what sign you should utilize. This is the place new dealers need a little assistance in understanding that all indicators work. The key to finding the best trading indicator lies not in finding the correct symbol, however instead in finding the perfect logo for you and your trading style.

The absolute most mainstream trading indicators incorporate RSI, MACD, Stochastic, and many, some more. These indicators and others can be utilized for trading. They will take a shot at any market and whenever outline, regardless of whether you don't swing exchange. Rather than looking for the best indicator, ask yourself what trading style you like and what you need or need from your sign. Indicators regularly show various parts of business sectors. Some are driving and caution of potential zones where the market might be overbought or oversold. A few signs are moving regular based, and instead, they plot the normal of cost on the diagram. If you comprehend what you need from an indicator, at that point, you can discover and begin exploring different avenues regarding signs of that sort. This will make finding the correct symbol for your trading style a lot simpler and quicker.

When you are trying and playing with trading indicators, dependably remember that no index is flawless. At the point when utilized appropriately, a sign can give you a trading advantage. Some new dealers make the presumption that the more symbols you place on your diagram, the better a broker you will be. This couldn't be any further from reality. It is suggested that you use all things considered three indicators at one time. When you begin utilizing any longer than this, you may find that your graphs become jumbled and that trading choices will turn out to be progressively troublesome. Usually, one indicator clashes with the sign of another that you are utilizing in the meantime. In this circumstance which trading indicator do you pursue? Keep it straightforward. Never use multiple symbols at once.

There are a lot of trading and swing trading indicators accessible. Finding the privilege or the best trading indicator probably won't be simple, however, you can rearrange the procedure by first choosing which type or what sort of data do you need your specialized sign to let you know. Would you like to know when the market might be depleted and preparing to pullback? Do you instead want to utilize moving midpoints of cost? When you recognize what you need, it will be anything but difficult to test and play with indicators of that sort until you locate the one that suits your style. Besides, dependably recall that more isn't in every case better. Keep your trading indicators on your diagram to a base. Utilizing any longer than three may make trading increasingly troublesome, and this is something no merchant should need.

Best Momentum Technical Indicators For Stocks

Momentum trading with stocks is a ground-breaking procedure that can be utilized without the worry of sitting for a long time gazing at a PC screen looking for each slight jerk in the market. It is helpful for medium-term stock trading, frames the establishment for fruitful swing trading, and opens up open doors for astounding benefits when utilizing choices trading techniques. The best part about momentum trading is that the requirement for broad information about specialized indicators isn't so high for what it's worth for swing trading or day trading. To be effective, it is ideal to stay with a couple of reliable indicators and fabricate your system from that.

What are the best Momentum Technical Indicators for Stocks?

Your eyes - you have to take a gander at a graph to discover how a stock is drifting. A figure does not let you know everything, except you, ought to have the option to identify an example just by taking a gander at the image of how the stock is moving. Every other indicator is accurate measures, and they possibly bode well when you can put them in a specific circumstance.

Moving midpoints. Two moving standard lines which are set for various timespans can be incredibly specialized indicators. For instance, at the same time utilizing a multi-day and multi-day exponential moving average (ema) lines can give an animated picture of how the momentum of a stock is streaming. When the ten ema line is over the multi-day line, at that point, it implies that throughout the previous ten days, the stock has been trading at a more expensive rate than throughout the last 30 days, by and large. It is in this manner in an upward pattern. You can apply these lines to the general market (Dow Jones, NASDAQ, and so forth.), or a segment, or your preferred stock.

More stunning's DMI or ADX is a measure to demonstrate the quality of the momentum. When it is over 25, in either heading, you can be confident that the energy is reliable and is probably going to hold.

Relative Strength Index (RSI) and Volatility Index (VIX) are the two indicators which show when an inversion in momentum is perhaps unavoidable. Both show when the market, by and large, is overbought or oversold and the RSI is useful for giving a similar data about a stock.

How to utilize these specialized indicators?

When you have set up that a pattern is set up, or that a stock is trading with momentum in a heading, you can:

- purchase a stock and hold it for the term of the pattern, or;

- exchange the swings here and there inside the trading band of the pattern, or;

- use choices trading methodologies; for example, credit spreads to adventure influence and get the most extreme benefit from a pattern.

What is the Best Swing Trading Indicator?

Swing merchants couldn't request substantially more than an indicator that could offer the opportunity of knowing ahead of time when the market they were trading was at its limit. If you could know ahead of time when a market was prepared to turn, this would extraordinarily expand your odds as a merchant of going into a gainful exchange. Fortunately, such indicators as of now exist, and when utilized appropriately, they offer to give you a colossal edge while trading. These indicators are known as momentum indicators.

While numerous indicators are slacking, momentum indicators are driving. Put; they offer a look at future value development before it has happened. Momentum indicators deal with the premise of estimating a cash pair's dimension of momentum. As a money pair backs off and lose speed or energy, the symbols caution of this and ready dealers that a likely retracement in future value development might be going to occur. By plotting a money pair's momentum, a merchant can know ahead of time when markets might plan to drawback.

One such momentum indicator is known as the RSI. The RSI (relative quality indicator) demonstrates dimensions of a cash pair that are considered overbought or oversold. At the point when the sign is in these zones, a merchant ought to be watchful for potential value retracement. At the point when a cash pair goes into overbought or oversold, there is a genuinely decent possibility that it will follow to conform to the new value levels before it proceeds. By knowing ahead of time when this may occur, brokers can finish exchanges off right on time and lock in benefits before they are cleaned away and always lost in the retracement.

If you need to know future value development ahead of time, at that point investigate momentum indicators, particularly the RSI, today. The RSI is one of the most established, and most confided in trading indicators accessible. This may be the trading indicator that you are searching for to give you an edge in your swing trading.

CONCLUSION

In the course of your trading experience, you must endeavor to learn from your experience which is the most effective way to master a skill. Although a mentor or a teacher can help you, you will soon find out that the most influential opinion when trading is your opinion so you must pay good attention to it and also make it good. How can you make your opinion good? You can do this by possessing the right mentality when entering any trade.

Whether the trade worked out or not, you must be ready to pick up yourself after losing a trade and focus again on the fact that you can make it again when trading next time. Having said that, you should also consider hiring a coach or get a mentor, someone who can always guide you in times you may experience difficulties in your trades.

I hope you have been able to learn some simple yet effective strategies that will help you achieve success in your swing trading journey. Remember, always adhere to your strategy and be disciplined when trading.